Coup d'État

Edward Luttwak

Coup d'Etat

A Practical Handbook

Harvard University Press
Cambridge, Massachusetts

To my father Josif Luttwak z.l.
And to my mother.

First published in Great Britain by Allen Lane
The Penguin Press 1968

This book has been digitally reprinted. The content
remains identical to that of previous printings.

Library of Congress Cataloging in Publication Data

Luttwak, Edward.
  Coup d'état: a practical handbook.

  Includes index.
  1. Coups d'état—Handbooks, manuals, etc.
I. Title.
JC494.L88   1979   321'.09   79–16525

ISBN 0–674–17547–6 pbk.

Printed in the United States of America

Contents

List of Figures

List of Tables

Foreword

Coup d'État, the brilliant and original book of a then very young man, first published in 1967, attracted immediate attention and appeared subsequently in the major languages. It is perhaps of even greater interest today, simply because it has become clearer during the last decade that far from being a fortunately rare exception in an otherwise civilized world order, the *coup d'état* is now the normal mode of political change in most member states of the United Nations. There are by now many more military dictatorships in existence than parliamentary democracies, and there are few cases on record in which such dictatorships have been overthrown by 'popular revolts'. Far more often the military men are replaced by one or more of their colleagues. Yet with all this there has been a virtual taboo on the study of *coup d'états,* and some critics of the present book obviously did not know quite what to make of it. It is in many ways easy to see why: the idea that a *coup d'état* can be carried out in many parts of the world with equal ease by small groups of men of the left and the right (and, for all one knows, also of the centre), provided they have mastered some elementary lessons of modern politics, is, of course, quite shocking. Marx and Engels wrote a great deal about revolution but hardly ever about the technique of revolution; the only nineteenth century left-wing leader who provided detailed instruction in this respect was Blanqui, and he was not very successful. There had been one other predecessor Gabriel Naudé, whose work was published in Paris in the late seventeenth century; an English translation by Dr. William King appeared in 1711 *(Political considerations upon Refined Politicks and the Master Strokes of State).* Some of this sounds very topical indeed:

> 'The thunderbolt falls before the noise of it is heard in the skies, prayers are said before the bell is rung for them; he receives the blow that thinks he himself is giving it, he suffers who never expected it, and he dies

that look'd upon himself to be the most secure; all is
done in the Night and Obscurity, amongst Storms and
Confusion.'

But Naudé has been forgotten for a long time, and his concept of
the 'master stroke' was, in any case, much wider than that of *coup
d'état* in its present meaning.

In our time whole libraries have been written on the objective
conditions in which revolutions take place, about civil and
peasant wars, about revolutionary and internal war, about guerrilla activities and terrorism, but almost nothing on *coup d'états*, and
this despite the fact that there have been few, if any, revolutions
of late and that 'objective conditions' are always only one of
several factors involved in their genesis. Seen in this light *coup
d'états* are annoying not only for practising politicians but also
from the point of view of the political scientist. For on the basis
of 'objective conditions' models and patterns can be built without undue difficulty, whereas *coups* are quite unpredictable,
almost by definition they are mortal enemies of orderly hypo-
theses and concepts: how does one account scientifically for
the political ambitions of a few strategically well placed individuals?

All this is highly regrettable but it does not lessen the need for
more thorough and detailed study of *coup d'états*. For according
to all indications this seems to be the 'wave of the future' – much
more than other, far more often discussed, forms of political
violence. A study of guerrilla warfare led me to the conclusion
that the army in most third world countries is the strongest
contender for domestic power: during the last fifteen years there
have been some hundred and twenty military *coups*, whereas only
five guerrilla movements have come to power – and three of these
followed the Portuguese *coup* in 1974. The function of the
guerrilla movement has reverted to what it originally was – that
of paving the way for and supporting the regular army: it holds
the stirrup so that others may get into the saddle, and the same
applies, *a fortiori* to terrorist groups. It is true that in some parts
of the world it has become more difficult to stage a military coup.
Once upon a time the commander of a tank brigade in a middle
Eastern country was at least a potential contender for political
power. This is no longer so, partly as the result of centralization
in military command, partly because the political police have
become more effective. But if in these parts *coups* have become

less frequent they are still the only form of political change that can be envisaged at the present time.

But even if *coups* are unpredictable, even if they defy known methods of interpretation (let alone of prediction), they contain certain ever recurring patterns – 'the same always different' – from the time the conspiracy is first hatched to the actual seizure of power. The present book is a major landmark in a field hitherto almost uncharted.

Walter Laqueur
Washington – London
October 1978

Preface to the First Edition

This is a handbook. It is therefore not concerned with a theoretical analysis of the *coup d'état*, but rather with the formulation of the techniques which can be employed to seize power within a state. It can be compared to a cookery book in the sense that it aims at enabling any layman equipped with enthusiasm – and the right ingredients – to carry out his own *coup*; only a knowledge of the rules is required. Two words of caution: in the first place in order to carry out a successful *coup* certain pre-conditions must be present, just as in cooking bouillabaisse one needs the right sorts of fish to start with. Secondly, readers should be aware that the penalty of failure is far greater than having to eat out of a tin. (The rewards, too, are greater.)

It may be objected that should such a handbook be inadequate or misleading the readers will be subject to great dangers, while if it is an efficient guide to the problems it may lead to upheavals and disturbances. My defence is that *coups* are already common and if, as a result of this book, a greater number of people learn how to carry them out this is merely a step towards democratization of the *coup* – a fact that all persons of liberal sentiments should applaud.

Finally, it should be noted that the techniques here discussed are politically neutral, and are only concerned with the objective of seizing control of the state, and not at all with subsequent policies. Readers interested in pursuing this subject further may wish to consult some of the standard academic works related to the subject, among which are: *The Role of the Military in Under-Developed Countries*, edited by J. J. Johnson, *The Man on Horseback*, by S. E. Finer, and the chapter on Armed Forces Organizations in Marion J. Levy Jr's *Modernization and Structure of Societies*.

E. L.

Preface to the 1979 Edition

During the years since the original publication of this book, I have frequently been told that it has served as the planning guide for this or that *coup*. But the only case of actual use for which there is firm evidence would make a poor advertisement: the *coup* in question was at first very successful but then failed, amidst much killing. Its chief protagonist, a defence minister who aspired to yet greater things, was caught and promptly executed. When his house was searched, a heavily annotated copy of the French edition was found in his study. I could take refuge in the excuse that the book's prescriptions were not followed with sufficient care, but in reality it was not my purpose to supply a *bona fide* do-it-yourself manual. In writing this book, my true aim was entirely different: to explore the meaning of political life in those backward countries now officially known as 'less developed'.

When the ideas in this book were first conceived, the intellectual classes of the Western world were passionately interested in the affairs of the Third World. There was an atmosphere of hopeful expectation about the new states of Africa and Asia, then emerging on the world scene for the first time. Even for Latin America there was a new interest, and new hopes – greatly stimulated by Kennedy's 'Alliance for Progress' which, like all of Kennedy's projects, enjoyed excellent publicity.

But it was undoubtedly Black Africa which stimulated the greatest interest, often remarkably emotional. The dissolution of the British and French empires was then still in progress, and the new states of Africa were the newest of all. Their utter poverty was not entirely concealed by the exotic scenery, and the almost complete absence of an educated class was brutally obvious. Yet it was only a few right-wing extremists, and the still smaller number of Old African Hands, who argued that independence was being granted too soon. This small minority was easily dismissed as reactionary and racist. The enlightened knew better:

the new states would muster the fresh energies of the peoples liberated from the lethargy of colonial rule; their youth would soon be educated to provide technicians, professionals and civil servants; given some aid from the West, a great upsurge of economic development was to be expected, and this would soon remedy backwardness, and the contrived poverty caused by colonial exploitation. More than that, we were told to look for moral leadership from the new states. The idealistic young leaders who had struggled for independence would be a great spiritual force on the world scene.

As a student at the London School of Economics the present writer heard such things being said as if they were not merely true but obvious. I had no desire to join the small band of right-wingers who alone, opposed the devolution of the British Empire. But I found the common view to be hopelessly removed from reality; our best minds seemed to suffer a decomposition of the critical faculties when the subject was the Third World. This is not the place to speculate on the obscure emotional reasons that alone could explain such a failure of the intellect. What is certain is that a highly favorable vision of the future of the Third World was given wide currency, even though all the factual evidence in hand flatly contradicted the notions on which the prediction was based.

It was not the poverty of the new states that made me dubious of their future, and entirely pessimistic as to their contribution to international life. Poverty does not necessarily inhibit cultural or even social achievement, and in any case some of the least promising of the new states already enjoyed vast unearned incomes from oil exports. As for the lack of adequate administrative structures, this was certainly not a fatal deficiency; few things grow as easily as state bureaucracies. Not even the ill-effects of relative deprivation felt by the poor, confronted with luxuries by way of the mass media, seemed to me to be all that serious. It seems that the 'revolution of rising expectations' – yet another slogan made by Western intellectuals to justify forthcoming depredations – has remained unrealized.

But there was one deficiency that was, and is, fatal, which would inevitably cause the new states to misgovern at home, while degrading international standards abroad. There was one thing that the new states lacked which they could neither make for themselves nor obtain from abroad, and this was a genuine political community. It is difficult to give a formal definition, and perhaps it is best to begin by evoking the familiar concept of the nation, in contrast to the state. The new states came into existence because the colonial authorities handed over their powers to political leaders who had agitated for independence; more specifically, the new leaders were given control over the army, police, tax collectors and administrators who had worked for the colonial government. The old servants of the empire served their new masters, ostensibly for new purposes. But their methods and their operational ideology were those of the imperial power, moulded by notions which reflected the values of *its* political community. There was no organic nexus between the native cultures and the instruments of state power, and neither could such a link be formed. For one thing there were usually several, quite different, native cultures, often incompatible. Moreover the methods and operational ideologies that the native cultures *would* organically sustain were usually utterly unsuited to the needs of modern life, that is Western life. The problem was not that this dissociation would make the state apparatus weak, but rather that it would leave it entirely unconstrained and much too strong. The consequences are now fully evident. The administrators of the new states are vested with all the great power over the individual that the entire machinery of files and records, vehicles, telecommunications and modern weapons give to the modern state. But their conduct is not constrained by legality, or by the moral standards which any genuine political community must enforce, even if only in requiring hypocrisy on the part of violators. Above all, their conduct is not restrained by political pressures, since the oppressed are neither afforded the electoral opportunities available in Western democracies, nor do they have social frameworks within which political action may be concerted. Hence the universal misgovernment which has replaced colonial non-government throughout the territories of the new states. Always present, bribery is now a quite normal part in any transaction between citizen and state; a detailed and pervasive oppression has replaced the distant authoritarianism of colonial days, since neither bureaucrats nor policemen are restrained by the rules of legality - or at least the procedures of legalism - which restrained the colonial power. As a result, exactions may increase without limit, and no citizen may assure his liberty, life or property by complying with the law - since the law offers no protection against the violations of its custodians. If colonialism was a crime, the greatest offence was in its undoing when fragile native cultures, embryonic modern societies, and minority peoples ill-provided to protect themselves, were everywhere abandoned into the hands of political leaders equipped with the powerful machine of the modern state. The brutalities of Idi Amin have been sufficiently spectacular to attract the persistent attention of Western media. But Idi Amin is fully justified in his complaint that the Western media are unfair to him: from Algeria to Zanzibar, the peoples of Africa are ruled by autocrats whose unfettered control over the machinery of the state allows them to indulge every vice and every excess of virtue: in one country the ruler may be an alcoholic, in another he may forbid alcoholic drink to all, because *he* deems it irreligious; in one country, the ruler may openly claim for himself any woman or boy that meets his fancy, in another he may have adulterers executed; in one country the most useless of luxuries may be freely imported while there is no foreign currency with which to buy essential medicines, in another the ruler may proclaim that even books may not be imported, although foreign currency is accumulating uselessly in foreign bank deposits. Above all, there is the systematic use of the instruments of defense and order for internal oppression, and the appropriation of public wealth on a fantastic scale. When the American Vice-President was forced to resign because he had accepted bribes, or what were deemed to be bribes, there was amazement at the size of the sums involved: in the Third World not even a junior minister could be purchased for so little. The logic whereby public power may easily generate privatte wealth is universal, and the enrichmen of the powerful is a pervasive phenomenon found all over the world. But there is a difference in the workings of this logic in the new states, and not merely of scale: it is not an ancillary phenomenon but rather the essential process of governance for those in control, and it is not moderated by the need for discretion. The overt corruption commonly found in the new states reveals the full consequences of the absence of political community. Only from the latter can effective norms arise, norms felt in the consciousness of each citizen. Without political community there can be no effective norms, and without the norms that arise quite naturally from the values and beliefs of the community, the state is no more than a machine. It is then that the *coup d'état* becomes feasible since, as with any machine, one may gain control over the whole by seizing hold of the critical levers. In writing of the *coup d'état* then, I was in fact writing of the true political life of the new states.

1. What is the *Coup d'État*?

'I shall be sorry to commence the era of peace by
a *coup d'état* such as that I had in contemplation.'
Duke of Wellington, 1811

'...no other way of salvation remained except for
the army's intervention ...' *Constantine Kollias,
21 April 1967, Athens*

Though the term *coup d'état* has been used for more than 300
years, the feasibility of the *coup* derives from a comparatively
recent development: the rise of the modern state with its professional bureaucracy and standing armed forces. The power of
the modern state largely depends on this permanent machinery
which, with its archives, files, records and officials, can follow
intimately and, if it so desires, control the activities of lesser
organizations and individuals. 'Totalitarian' states merely use
more fully the detailed and comprehensive information which is
available to most states, however 'democratic': the instrument is
largely the same though it is used differently.

The growth of the modern bureaucracy has two implications
which are crucial to the feasibility of the *coup*: the development
of a clear distinction between the permanent machinery of state
and the political leadership, and the fact that, like most large
organizations, the bureaucracy has a structured hierarchy with
definite chains of command. The distinction between the
bureaucrat as an employee of the state and as a personal servant
of the ruler is a new one, and both the British and the American
systems show residual features of the earlier structure.*

*In Britain there is the constitutional fiction that civil servants – as their
name implies – are the servants of the Crown. In the USA, while the days
when party hacks moved on to Washington after an election victory are long
past, some civil-service jobs are still given to political associates, rather
than to professionals.

The importance of this development lies in the fact that if the bureaucrats are linked to the leadership, an illegal seizure of power must take the form of a 'Palace Revolution' and it essentially concerns the manipulation of the person of the ruler. He can be forced to accept new policies or advisers, he can be killed or held captive, but whatever happens the Palace Revolution can only be conducted from the 'inside', and by 'insiders'. The 'insiders' can be the palace guard as in ancient Rome, or the Ethiopia of the 1960s, and in a dynastic system they would seek to replace an unwanted ruler with a more malleable son.

The *coup* is a much more democratic affair. It can be conducted from the 'outside' and it operates in that area outside the government but within the state which is formed by the permanent and professional civil service, the armed forces and police. The aim is to detach the permanent employees of the state from the political leadership, and this cannot usually take place if the two are linked by political, ethnic or traditional loyalties.

Both Imperial China and present-day African states use ethnic bonds in the organization of their senior bureaucracy. The Manchu dynasty was careful to follow native Chinese customs and to employ 'Han' Chinese in the civil service at all levels, but the crucial posts in the magistracy and the army were filled by the descendants of those who entered China with the founders of the dynasty. Similarly, African rulers usually appoint members of their own tribes to the strategic posts in the security services.

When a party machine controls civil-service appointments, either as part of a general 'totalitarian' control, or because of a very long period in office (as in post-war Italy), political associates are appointed to the senior levels of the bureaucracy, partly in order to protect the regime and partly to ensure the sympathetic execution of policies. Thus 'party men' hold the key jobs in the police and security services of France and Italy, just as in the communist countries all senior jobs are held by party *'apparatchiks'*.

Saudi Arabia provides an instance of 'traditional bonds'.* In

---

*The bonds are religious in origin since the Saudi royal house is the traditional promoter of the Wahabi interpretation of Islam.

this case the lack of modern 'know-how' on the part of the traditional tribal affiliates of the royal house has meant that what could not be done individually has been done organizationally. Alongside the modern army staffed by unreliable city-dwellers, there is the 'White Army' of the Wahabi bedouin followers of the Saudis.

Such possible bonds between political leadership and the bureaucracy are not typical of the modern state. Apart from the cases noted above, the civil service and the leadership of the modern state may still be linked by class or ethnic affiliations, but whatever the nature of the bonds, such groupings will usually be large enough to be infiltrated by the planners of the *coup.*

As a direct consequence of the sheer size of the bureaucracy, and in order to achieve even a minimum of efficiency, the state bureaucracy has to divide its work into clear-cut areas of competence, which are assigned to different departments. Within each department there must be an accepted chain of command, and standard procedures have to be followed. Thus a given piece of information, or a given order, is followed up in a stereotyped manner, and if the order comes from the appropriate source, at the appropriate level, it is carried out.

In the more critical parts of the state apparatus, the armed forces, the police, and the security services, all these charac-teristics are intensified, with an even greater degree of discipline and rigidity. The apparatus of the state is therefore to some extent a 'machine' which will normally behave in a fairly predictable and automatic manner.

A *coup* operates by taking advantage of this machine-like behaviour: during the *coup* because it uses parts of the state apparatus to seize the controlling levers; afterwards because the value of the 'levers' depends on the fact that the state is a machine.

We will see that some states are so well organized that the 'machine' is sufficiently sophisticated to exercise discretion, according to a given conception of what is 'proper' and what is not, in the orders that it executes. This is the case in some developed countries, and in such circumstances a *coup* is very difficult to carry out.

In a few states the bureaucracy is so small that the apparatus is too simple and too intimately linked with the leadership to be suitable for a *coup*, as perhaps in the ex-British Protectorates in southern Africa, Botswana, Lesotho and Swaziland. Fortunately, most states are between these two extremes, the machine being both large and unsophisticated and thus highly vulnerable to those who can identify and seize the right 'levers'.

One of the most striking developments of the last century has been the great decline in general political stability. Since the French Revolution governments have been overthrown at an increasing pace.* In the nineteenth century the French experienced two revolutions and two regimes collapsed following military defeat. In 1958 the change of regime was a sophisticated blend of both these elements. Peoples everywhere have followed the French example, and the life-span of regimes has tended to decrease while the life-span of their subjects has increased. This contrasts sharply with the relative attachment to the system of constitutional monarchy which was displayed in the nineteenth century: when Greeks, Bulgars and Rumanians secured their freedom from the Turkish colonial system they immediately went over to Germany in order to shop around for a suitable royal family.

Crowns, flags and decorations were designed and purchased from reputable (English) suppliers; royal palaces were built; and where possible, hunting lodges, royal mistresses, and a local aristocracy were provided as fringe benefits. Twentieth-century peoples have, on the other hand, shown a marked lack of interest in monarchies and their paraphernalia; when the British kindly provided them with a proper royal family the Iraqis made numerous efforts to get rid of it, before finally succeeding in 1958. Military and other right-wing forces have meanwhile tried to keep up with popular movements and have used their illegal methods in order to seize power and overthrow regimes.

*Historically speaking, the trend was initiated by the American Revolution; its impact on the world at large was, however, attenuated by America' distance and exotic nature.

Why have regimes in the twentieth century proved so fragile? It is, after all, paradoxical that this fragility has increased while the established procedures for securing changes in government have on the whole become more flexible. The political scientist will reply that though the procedures have become more flexible, pressures for change have also become stronger, and that the rate of increase in flexibility has not kept up with the growth of social and economic pressures.*

Violent methods are generally used when legal methods of securing a governmental change are useless because they are either too rigid – as in the case of ruling monarchies where the ruler actually controls policy formation – or not rigid enough. It was once remarked, for example, that the throne of Russia was, until the seventeenth century, neither hereditary nor elective but 'occupative'. The long series of abdications forced by the great Boyar-landlords and by the 'Archers' of the Guard had weakened the hereditary principle, so that whoever took the throne became Tzar, and precedence by birth counted for little.

Some contemporary republics have ended in this position, which comes about when a long series of illegal seizures of power leads to a decay of the legal and political structures which are needed to produce new governments. Thus post-war Syria has had more than a dozen *coups,* and the provisions for open general elections, written in the 'Hourani' constitution, could not now be applied because the necessary supervisory machinery no longer functions. Assuming, however, that there is an established procedure for changing the leadership, then all methods other than this come within the range of illegality. What we call them† depends on what side we are on but, skipping some of the semantics, we have the following:

*Perhaps the ultimate source of destabilizing pressures has been the spectacular progress of scientific discovery and the resultant technological change. This is, however, a problem far beyond the scope of this book.

†The equation 'Insurgency = Terrorism = War of National Liberation' is particularly familiar.

Revolution

The action is conducted, initially at any rate, by uncoordinated popular masses, and it aims* at changing the social and political structures, as well as the actual personalities in the leadership.

The term has gained a certain popularity, and many *coups* are graced with it, because of the implication that it was 'the people' rather than a few plotters who did the whole thing. Thus the obscure aims which Kassem had in mind when he overthrew the Faisal-Nuri-es-Said regime in Iraq are locally known as the 'sacred principles of the July 14th Revolution'.

Civil War

Civil War is actual warfare between elements of the national armed forces leading to the displacement of a government.

This term is unfashionable and if you are Spanish and pro-Franco you call the events of 1936–9 *'la cruzada'* – the crusade. If you are not pro-Franco, but you may be overheard, you just call them 'the events of . . .'

Pronunciamiento

This is an essentially Spanish and South American version of the military *coup d'état*, but many recent African *coups* have also taken this particular form. In its original nineteenth-century Spanish version this was a highly ritualized process: first came the *trabajos* (literally the 'works') in which the opinions of army officers were sounded. The next step was the *compromisos*, in which commitments were made and rewards promised; then came the call for action and, finally, the appeal to the troops to follow their officers in rebellion against the government.

The *pronunciamiento* was often a liberal rather than a reactionary phenomenon and the theoretical purpose of the take-over was to ascertain the 'national will' – a typically liberal

*In the initial stages no aims are conceptualized but the scope of the action may be clearly perceived.

concept. Later, as the army became increasingly right-wing while Spanish governments became less so, the theory shifted from the neo-liberal 'national will' to the neo-conservative 'real will' theory. This postulates the existence of a national essence, a sort of permanent spiritual structure, which the wishes of the majority may not always express. The army was entrusted with the interpretation and preservation of this 'essential Spain' and to protect it against the government and, if need be, against the people.*

The *pronunciamiento* was organized and led by a particular army leader, but it was carried out in the name of the entire officer corps; unlike the *putsch*, which is carried out by a faction within the army, or the *coup*, which can be carried out by civilians *using* some army units, the *pronunciamiento* leads to a take-over by the army as a whole. Many African take-overs, in which the army has participated as a whole, were therefore very similar to the classic *pronunciamiento*.

Putsch

Essentially a wartime or immediately post-war phenomenon, a *putsch* is attempted by a formal body within the armed forces under its appointed leadership. The Kornilov *putsch* is a clear example: Kornilov, a general in charge of an army group in north Russia, attempted to seize Leningrad, in order to establish a 'fighting' regime which would prosecute the war. (Had he succeeded, the city would perhaps bear his name instead of Lenin's.)

Liberation

A state may be said (by supporters of the change) to be 'liberated when its government is overthrown by foreign military or diplomatic intervention. A classic case of this was the installation of the Communist leadership in Rumania in 1947. The USSR forced the then King Michael to accept a new Cabinet by

*Various versions of this theory became popular in parts of the French Armed Forces during the 1950s and early 1960s.

threatening to use the Soviet army in the country in the event of a refusal.

War of National Liberation, Insurgency etc.

In this form of internal conflict the aim of the initiating party is not to seize power within the state, but rather to set up a rival state structure. This can be politically or ethnically based.

The Viet Cong in South Vietnam aim at setting up a new social structure and, incidentally, a new state. The Kurds in Iraq, the Somalis in Kenya, the Karens in Burma and the Nagas in India want to withdraw their areas from the state concerned.

The Definition of the Coup

A *coup d'état* involves some elements of all these different methods by which power can be seized but, unlike most of them, the *coup* is not necessarily assisted by either the intervention of the masses, or, to any significant degree, by military-type force.

The assistance of these forms of direct force would no doubt make it easier to seize power, but it would be unrealistic to think that they would be available to the organizers of a *coup*. Because we will not be in charge of the armed forces we cannot hope to start the planning of a *coup* with sizeable military units already under our control, nor will the pre-*coup* government usually allow us to carry out the propaganda and organization necessary to make effective use of the 'broad masses of the people'.

A second distinguishing feature of a *coup* is that it does not imply any particular political orientation. Revolutions are usually 'leftist' while the *putsch* and the *pronunciamiento* are usually initiated by right-wing forces. A *coup*, however, is politically neutral, and there is no presumption that any particular policies will be followed after the seizure of power. It is true that many *coups* have been of a decidedly right-wing character but there is nothing inevitable about this.*

---

*The Greek *coup* has reinforced this image of the 'reactionary *coup*' but the Syrian *coup* of 1966, the Iraqi of 1958, the Yemeni of 1962 were all essentially leftist, if hardly liberal or progressive.

If a *coup* does not make use of the masses, or of warfare, what instrument of power will enable it to seize control of the state? The short answer is that the power will come from the state itself. The long answer makes up the bulk of this book. The following is our formal and functional definition:

A *coup* consists of the infiltration of a small but critical segment of the state apparatus, which is then used to displace the government from its control of the remainder.

2. When is a *Coup d'État* Possible?

'The Bolsheviks have no right to wait for the
Congress of Soviets. . . . They must take power
immediately. . . . Victory is assured and there are
nine chances out of ten that it will be bloodless.
. . . To wait is a crime against the revolution.'
Vladimir Ilich Ulyanov Lenin, October 1917

Since 1945, the process of decolonization has more than doubled
the number of independent states, so that the opportunities open
to us have expanded in a most gratifying manner. We have to
recognize, however, that not all states make good targets for our
attentions. There is nothing to prevent us from carrying out a
coup in, say, Britain, but we would probably be unable to stay in
power for more than a short time. The public and the bureaucracy have a basic understanding of the nature and legal basis of
government and they would react in order to restore a legitimate
leadership.

This reaction renders any initial success of the *coup* meaning-
less, and it would arise even though the pre-*coup* government
may have been unpopular, and the 'new faces' might be
attractive. The reaction would arise from the fact that a significant part of the population takes an active interest in political
life, and participates in it. This implies a recognition that the
power of the government derives from its legitimate origin, and
even those who have no reason to support the old guard have
many good reasons to support the principle of legitimacy.

We are all familiar with the periodic surveys which 'show'
that, say, twenty per cent of the sample failed to name correctly
the Prime Minister, and we know that a large part of the
population has only the vaguest contact with politics. Nevertheless in most developed countries those who *do* take an active
interest in politics form in absolute terms a very large group.

Controversial policy decisions stimulate and bring to the surface this participation: pressure groups are formed, letters are sent to the press and the politicians, petitions and demonstrations are organized, and this adds up to a continuing dialogue between the rulers and the ruled.

This dialogue does not depend necessarily on the existence of a formally democratic political system. Even in one-party states, where power is in the hands of a few self-appointed leaders, a muted but nevertheless active dialogue can take place. The higher organizations of the party can discuss policy decisions, and in times of relative relaxation the discussions extend to the larger numbers in the lower echelons, and to publications reflecting different 'currents' – though only within the wider framework of the accepted ideology and the broad policy decisions of the leadership. The value of the dialogue that takes place in non-democratic states varies very greatly. In Yugoslavia,* for example, the Communist Party has become a forum for increasingly free and wide-ranging debates on major political issues; the press and the parliament, though unable to assert their opinions in the manner of their American or British counterparts, have also participated in the 'opening' of the system. Policy decisions are no longer merely applauded but are actually examined, criticized, and sometimes even opposed.

It may well be that this particular one-party state is no longer good *coup* territory. When people have learned to scrutinize and question orders they will probably refuse merely to *accept* the orders of the *coup*, any more than they accept the orders of the government without ascertaining their legitimacy and desirability.

In Egypt, on the other hand, the single party, the Arab Socialist Union (the ASU), is still a mere rubber stamp. Policy decisions are made by Abd-el-Nasir† and his associates; they are then carried out by the bureaucracy, and the ASU can only cheer them along. When the question came up of whether the ASU-dominated National Assembly would accept Nasir's with-

---

*And of late in Czechoslovakia.

†Abd-el-Nasir = Servant of the Giver of Victory. Nasir or Nas*ser* means Victory, and this is rather inappropriate.

drawal of his 'resignation', following the June 1967 débâcle, an observer pointed out that the Assembly 'will jolly well do what it is told'. Many one-party states are in this position.

The dialogue between the rulers and the ruled can only take place if there is a large enough section of society which is sufficiently literate, well fed and secure to 'talk back'. Even then certain conditions can lead to a deterioration of the relationship, and this can sometimes generate sufficient apathy and distrust of the regime to make a *coup* possible.

The events of 1958 in France were in some respects similar to a *coup*. Twenty years of warfare, which had included the defeat of 1940, the Occupation and, from 1946, the long and losing colonial wars in Indochina and Algeria, had undermined the political structure. The continual changes of government had lost for the regime the interest and respect of most Frenchmen and left the bureaucracy leaderless, since the complex business of the ministries could not be mastered by ministers who were only in power for brief periods. The military were left to fight the bitter Algerian war with little guidance from the Paris authorities, because more often than not, the ministries were too busy fighting for their survival in the Assembly to worry about the other, bloodier, war.

The cost of the war, in both money and lives, antagonized the general public from both the army and the government, and many Frenchmen felt a growing fear and distrust of this army, whose sentiments and ideology was so alien to them – and to the spirit of the times.

While the structures of political life under the IVth Republic were falling apart, de Gaulle, in simulated retirement, gradually emerged as the only alternative to the chaos that threatened. When the army in Algeria appeared to be on the verge of really drastic action – far beyond the earlier street theatricals of Algiers – and yet another government was on the verge of collapse, de Gaulle was recalled.

He was able to impose his own terms. When on 29 May 1958 Coty, the last President of the IVth Republic, called on him to form a government (which was invested on 1 June), de Gaulle was given powers to rule by decree for six months and to write a new constitution. Under the terms of this constitution, presented for consultation in mid-August and approved by referendum in September, elections were held in which de Gaulle's newly formed UNR party won a majority. On 21 December de Gaulle became the first President of the Vth Republic – an American-style President with wide executive powers, but without an American-style Congress to restrain them.

The France of 1958 had become politically inert and therefore ripe for a *coup*. The political structures of most developed countries, however, are too resilient to make them suitable targets, unless certain 'temporary' factors weaken the system and obscure its basic soundness. Of those temporary factors the most common are:

(*a*) severe and prolonged economic crisis, with large-scale unemployment or runaway inflation;

(*b*) a long and unsuccessful war or a major defeat, military or diplomatic;

(*c*) chronic instability under a multi-party system.

Italy is an interesting example of an economically developed, socially dynamic, but politically fragile country. Until the formation of the present relatively stable coalition between the *Democrazia Cristiana* (DC) and the Socialists, the DC – though the largest single party – could only rule by allying itself with some of the many small parties of the centre, as it rarely polled more than a simple majority.*

Coalition governments are always difficult to form, and in Italy the problem became so complex that it resembled a particularly intricate puzzle. If you had been called to form a government you would have been facing a set of mutually exclusive propositions:

The DC is the single largest group in Parliament but, having only thirty per cent of the votes, it cannot rule alone. If the two small left-of-centre parties (the Social Democrats and the Republicans) are brought in, the right-wing breaks away and the government falls. If the right-of-centre parties (the Monarchists and the Liberals) are brought in, the left-wing

*The stable coalition has since collapsed.

breaks away and the government falls. If the large far-right-wing party (the Neo-Fascists) is brought in, all the left-wing groups will vote against the government. If . . .

So the ruling party has stayed in power since 1948 without a break, but it has not been able to do so at the same time reforming the swollen and inefficient bureaucracy. Everybody wanted reform, except that the right-wing resisted changes in the structure of local government and the police, while the left opposed any checks on the fantastic activities of the State corporation.* Meanwhile the parties out of power concentrated their efforts on trying to break the coalition rather than on scrutinizing governmental policy, so that abuses and inefficiency were unchecked.

Italians gradually lost interest in the goings-on in Rome, and had there been an Italian de Gaulle the Republic would no doubt have collapsed. (Even without a suitable man a *coup* almost took place.)

The Pre-Conditions of the Coup

The France of 1958 and, to a lesser extent, the Italy of 1964 were both countries where the dialogue between government and people had broken down. But in many – indeed most – countries of the world the dialogue cannot take place at all, regardless of the temporary circumstances.

If we draw up a list of those countries which have recently experienced *coups*, we shall see that though their ethnic and historical backgrounds differ very considerably, they share certain social and economic characteristics. If we isolate these we can develop a set of indicators which when applied to the basic socio-economic data of a country will show whether it will make a good target for a *coup*.

---

*The activities of Enrico Mattei, the head of the National Hydrocarbon Corporation (ENI) have been described in almost Bondian terms in a number of books; he built up an industrial empire, battled the international oil industry, interfered in Italian politics, forced foreign policy changes, and died in unexplained circumstances.

ECONOMIC BACKWARDNESS

In countries without a developed economy and the associated prosperity, the general condition of the population is characterized by disease, illiteracy, high birth- and death-rates, and periodic hunger.

The average man in this state of deprivation is virtually cut off from the wider society outside his village and clan. He has little that he can sell. He has little with which to buy. He cannot read the forms, signposts and newspapers through which society speaks to him. He cannot write, nor can he afford to travel, so that a cousin living as a city-dweller might as well be on the moon. He has no way of knowing whether a particular tax is legal, or merely the exaction of the village bureaucrat; no way of knowing about the social and economic realities that condition the policies that he is asked to applaud. His only source of contact with the outside world is the governmental radio – and he knows from past experience that it does not always tell the truth.

The complexity of the outside world and the mistrust that it inspires are such that the defenceless and insecure villager retreats into the safe and well-known world of the clan, the tribe or the family. He knows that the traditional chiefs of tribe and clan prey on his very limited wealth, he often knows that their mutual interests are diametrically opposed, but nevertheless they represent a source of guidance and security that the state is too remote and too mysterious, to be.

The city-dweller has escaped the crushing embrace of traditional society, but not the effects of ignorance and insecurity. In these conditions the mass of the people is politically passive and its relationship with the leadership is one-way only. The leadership speaks to them, lectures them, rouses hopes or fears, but never listens; the bureaucracy taxes them, bullies them, takes their sons away for the army, their labour for the roads, but gives very little in return. At best, in honest regimes, a dam or a steel mill is being built somewhere, far away from their village. These projects will not bring them any direct benefit, will not lift them from their misery, but at least they are a consolation, a hope of a better future for their sons. Elsewhere the poor are even denied the consolation of hope: their taxes have been spent on palaces, tanks, planes, and all the bizarre things that politicians and their wives need. The urban poor living by expedients, barely surviving in the day-to-day struggle for the necessities of life, are treated to the spectacle of the cocktail parties, limousines and grandiose villas of the ruling *élite*.*

The mass of the people is politically passive, but it is the passivity of enforced silence, not inertia. All the time the terrible anger caused by deprivation and injustice is there, and at times it explodes. The mob may not have a clear political purpose, but its actions do have political consequences.

The 1952 *coup* in Egypt, which led to the end of King Farouk's 'white telephone' monarchy, and to the rise of what eventually became Abd-el-Nasir's regime, was preceded by one of these sudden explosions. 26 January 1952 ('Black Saturday') was the appointed date of an organized demonstration against the presence and activities of the British forces in the Canal Zone. The poor of the city streamed out from their hovels and joined the procession, amongst them the agitators of the Muslim Brotherhood,† who incited the crowd to arson and violence.

The agitators succeeded beyond their wildest dreams. The poor seized the opportunity and destroyed the facilities of the rich: hotels, department stores, the Turf Club, the liquor stores and fashion shops in the centre of the city which was given the appearance of a battlefield in one short day; only the wealthy suffered, as these were places that had always been closed to the poor. The middle-class organizers of the original demonstration had no wish to destroy their own favourite gathering places; the nationalists did not want to deprive Egypt of the 12,000 dwellings and 500 businesses that were destroyed. They spoke of anarchy, intrigue and madness. For the poor, however, it was a general election: the voteless poor had voted with fire.

*Even then some of them retain their sense of humour; in some African languages a new word has been coined from the Wa-prefix which indicates a tribe, and where before there were only Wa-Kamba and Wa-Zungu now a new tribe has appeared: the Wa-Benz and the Wa-Rolls-Royce.

†As in all Middle Eastern episodes, the affiliations of the agitators are not certain. It has been said that the Palace organized the whole thing.

Apart from the violent and inarticulate action of the mob in response to some simple and dramatic issue, there is no arguing with the power of the state; there is no interest in, and scrutiny of, the day-to-day activities of government and bureaucracy. Thus if the bureaucracy issues orders they are either obeyed or evaded, but never challenged or examined.

All power, all participation, is in the hands of the small educated *élite*. This *élite* is literate, educated, well-fed and secure, and therefore radically different from the vast majority of their countrymen, practically a race apart. The masses recognize this and they also accept the *élite*'s monopoly of power, and unless some unbearable exaction leads to desperate revolt they will accept its policies. *Equally they will accept a change in government, whether legal or otherwise.* After all, it is merely another lot of 'them' taking over.

Thus, after a *coup*, the village policeman comes to read out a proclamation, the radio says that the old government was corrupt and that the new one will provide food, health, schooling – and sometimes even glory. The majority of the people will neither believe nor disbelieve these promises or accusations, but merely feel that it is all happening somewhere else, far away. This lack of reaction★ is all the *coup* needs on the part of the people in order to stay in power.

The lower levels of the bureaucracy will react – or rather fail to react – in a similar manner, and for similar reasons. Their own lack of political sophistication will mean that the policies and legitimacy of the old government were much less important to them than their immediate superiors. The 'bosses' give the orders, can promote or demote and, above all, are the source of that power and prestige that make them village demi-gods. After the *coup*, the man who sits at district headquarters will still be obeyed – whether he is the man who was there before or not – so long as he can pay the salaries and has links to the political stratosphere in the capital city.

★The crowds that demonstrated in Cairo to dissuade Nasir from resigning on 10 June 1967 gave impressive proof of his popularity. This was not, however, an *independent* reaction: peasants from the Delta had been trucked by the thousand to 'stimulate' the demonstration, which was widely publicized by the state broadcasting service.

For the senior bureaucrats, army and police officers, the *coup* will be a mixture of dangers and opportunities. Some will be too compromised with the old regime merely to ride out the crisis and they will either flee, fight the *coup*, or step forward as supporters of the new regime in order to gain the rewards of early loyalty. The course of action followed by this group will depend on their individual assessments of the balance of forces on the two sides. But for the greater number of those who are not too deeply committed, the *coup* will offer opportunities rather than dangers. They can accept the *coup* and, being collectively indispensable, can negotiate for even better salaries and positions; they can create or join a focus of opposition; or, as in Nigeria in 1966, can take advantage of the temporary state of instability and stage a counter-*coup* and seize power on their own account.

Much of the planning and execution of a *coup* will be directed at influencing the decision of the *élite* in a favourable manner. Nevertheless if, in an underdeveloped environment, they choose to oppose the *coup*, they will have to do so in terms of political rivalry. They would not be able to appeal to some general principle of legality as in politically sophisticated countries, because no such principle is generally accepted. So instead of operating for the sake of legitimacy, they would be fighting the planners of the *coup* as straight political opponents and therefore on the same plane. This would have the effect of bringing over to the *coup their* political or ethnic opponents. In any case, fighting the *coup* would mean facing organized forces with improvised ones, and in conditions of isolation from the masses who, as we have seen, will almost always be neutral.*

As the *coup* will not usually represent a threat to most of the *élite*, the choice is between the great dangers of opposition and the safety of inaction. All that is required in order to support the *coup* is, simply, to do nothing – and this is what will usually be done.

---

*Many observers have commented on the lack of popular support for fallen political idols, as in the case of N'krumah's overthrow when the Accra citizenry seemed as happy to cheer his enemies as they had been to cheer him shortly before the *coup*. This is not inanity, but highly rational behaviour in the light of social and economic circumstances.

Thus, at all levels, the most likely course of action following a *coup* is acceptance: by the masses and the lower bureaucracy because their interests are not tied with either side; by the upper levels of the bureaucracy because of the great dangers of any opposition conducted in isolation. This lack of reaction is the key to the victory of the *coup*, and it contrasts with the spontaneous reaction that would take place in politically sophisticated societies.

In totalitarian states the midnight arrests, the control over all associations (however non-political), are all part of the general tactic of insulating the individual who seeks to oppose the regime. In underdeveloped areas the opposition is isolated from the masses almost automatically by the effect of social conditions.

Our first pre-condition of a *coup* is therefore:

The social and economic conditions of the target country must be such as to confine political participation to a small fraction of the population.

By participation we do not mean an active and prominent role in national politics, but merely that general understanding of the basis of political life, commonly found amongst the masses in economically developed societies. This pre-condition also implies that, apart from the highest levels, the bureaucracy operates in an unresponsive and mechanical manner because of its under-educated staff.

More generally the 'economic pre-condition' excludes the possibility of a system of local government – or rather representative local government. It is true that in underdeveloped areas there is often a system of local government, based on traditional chiefs, but of their two possible roles, neither usually functions as a representative one.* They are either individually powerful in their own right, which means in effect that the commoner is subjected to dual control, or else if their power has collapsed they are little more than somewhat old-fashioned civil servants. Neither of these two roles allows the commoner to

*There are some tribal groupings in Africa (notably the Kabyles of Algeria) and elsewhere where an almost pure 'Greek city' type of democracy exists. But they are exceptions to the rule.

participate in the small politics of the village or town in the manner of his Western counterpart.

Thus, in an economically backward environment the diffusion of power, which is characteristic of sophisticated democracies, cannot take place. There is either rigid centralized rule, or, as a transitional phase, a degree of power for individual regions that makes them *de facto* independent states (as was the case in northern Nigeria before the *coup*). Everybody knows that it is easier to take something concrete than something vague. Talking loosely, power in the centralized state run by a narrow *élite* is like a well-guarded treasure; power in a sophisticated democracy is like a free-floating atmosphere – and who can seize that?

The pre-condition of economic backwardness can be tested against the known facts of the degree of economic development of countries that have had *coups* in the last ten years or so and there is a clear connexion between the two.*

This does not necessarily mean that (a) all underdeveloped countries are *ipso facto* vulnerable to a *coup*, nor (b) that the developed areas are never good *coup* territory. It does mean however, that only the intervention of special circumstances will prevent a well-planned *coup* from succeeding in economically backward countries, while only exceptional circumstances (discussed in Chapter 1) will allow it to succeed in the developed areas.

POLITICAL INDEPENDENCE

It is impossible to seize power within a state if the major source of political power is not there to be seized. The 1956 Hungarian Revolution, for example, was totally successful and the leaders of the Revolution quickly found themselves in control of all the traditional instruments of power: the armed forces, the police, the radio and the communication facilities. The one thing that could not be seized in the streets of Budapest happened to be the major source of power to the previous regime: the presence of the Soviet Army in and around Hungary.

*See Appendix C, Table I.

These armed forces – vastly superior to the Hungarian Army – were a greater source of power to a Kremlin-backed government than any element within the country. The control of the Red Army was in Moscow, thus the Revolution would only have succeeded if it had been carried out in Moscow, not Budapest.*

This dependence of one government on another is a widespread phenomenon; although there are very few colonial states left there are many pseudo-independent ones. In some cases these have less real autonomy than some of the old colonies.

In both East Germany and South Vietnam the armed forces of the greater 'ally' are much more powerful than those of the country itself. In both countries the international and the domestic situations are so closely interrelated that the greater 'ally' must have effective control over vast areas of domestic policy – even assuming that he had no wish to interfere for other reasons. The rulers of East Germany have always been very careful in ensuring the approval of the Soviet authorities for even the smallest policy changes, and each policy announcement can be traced back to a recent trip to Moscow. Similarly, in Saigon the US embassy is generally recognized as a greater source of power than the Presidential Palace.

In these conditions a *coup* can only work with the approval of the greater 'ally'. The first *coup* in Vietnam, which overthrew the unpopular Diem, and the still less popular Ngo family, was carried out by men who appreciated these realities of power. When the events of Hué of 8 May 1963 resulted in a break between Diem and the Buddhists, the long-suffering generals decided to act: they 'sounded out' the opinion of the US embassy in Saigon, and asked through an intermediary whether the Americans would report to Diem 'possible consultations on eventual changes in the prevailing political structures'. When, after some considerable debate between the CIA, the embassy, the Presidency and the Pentagon, the US authorities informed the plotters that they would not be reported to Diem, the following sequence of events took place:

*The other cause of the failure of the Revolution was, of course, the fact that Moscow's intervention was not stopped by Washington but, again the control of US policy cannot be seized in Budapest.

May 1963: Beginning of intensified conflict between Buddhists and Diem.

May–September: Internal American debate on whether the Buddhists are neutralists (to be opposed) or nationalists (to be supported). The final conclusion reached was that 'Hinayana Buddhists' were 'bad' and 'Mahayana* Buddhists' were 'good'.

October 1963: Standstill of all economic aid to Vietnam, i.e. to Diem's regime.

22 October 1963: End of direct aid by CIA to Ngo Dinh Nhu's† 'Special Forces'. These were the main source of direct power to the regime, entirely financed and equipped by the CIA.

1 November 1963: *Coup.* 2 November: death of Diem and Ngo Dinh Nhu.

The Viet Cong accused the generals and their 'front-man', Van Minh, of being stooges of the Americans, but in their dealings with the US authorities they were merely being realistic: they saw that whatever power there was to be seized depended on the Americans. Seizing Saigon's fixtures and fittings without US support would have been seizing an empty symbol.

East Germany and South Vietnam are two clear cases of dependence, but there are many more countries which are in the grey area between effective independence and total submission. Ex-colonies provide many of these more subtle cases of dependence, and the presence of the former mother-country is very real, and very effective. Instead of large and expensive armies there are military and economic 'advisers', there is economic aid and, above all, the tight web of long-established dependence in non-political areas. Thus schooling follows patterns originally established in colonial days, the organization of the professions follows the 'metropolitan' system, and this is very important where the ruling *élite* is composed largely of lawyers, whose whole *raison d'être* is based on the use of a particular procedure and code of law. Trade is often largely tied to the ex-colonial power because of the hold of inherited tastes, habits,

*See *Buddhism* by Christmas Humphries (Penguin Books, 1951). For a fuller discussion of Buddhism in South Vietnamese politics see Chapter 4.

†Diem's brother-in-law and sometime 'strong man' of South Vietnam.

and the fact that trade links are often based on established relationships and communications. Thus, five years after independence, it was still necessary for adjacent ex-French and ex-British colonies to route telephone calls through Paris and London, though a direct line would have been 300 instead of 5,000 miles long.

The power of these links between ex-colonies and the former colonial power varies from case to case. But quite unobtrusive ties can sometimes give sufficient leverage to the latter to prevent or oppose a *coup*. Thus in 1964 the French reversed an otherwise successful *coup* in Gabon – without needing to use more than symbolic force. The power of the ex-colonial countries has waned from its peak in most places, but it is still considerable even in sheer military terms. Everybody remembers how a few companies of commandos stopped the mutinies in East Africa. Although the French have opted for a policy of neutrality to new *coups* in Gabon and elsewhere, should they want to intervene they still (1968) retain six thousand troops in Africa, with air transport and efficient equipment.* Six thousand does not sound like a large force, but it is huge compared to most armies in the ex-French colonies – the Central African Republic's army, for example, numbers 500 and the average for the whole group is about a battalion (1,000 men) per country.

A very specialized type of dependence is a by-product of modern technology and is found outside the ex-colonial sphere. This is the heavy mortgage placed on political independence by the acquisition of sophisticated weaponry, particularly aircraft. The jet fighter is the crucial case: unlike ships and tanks, jet fighters confer an absolute advantage. Better training and morale can overcome the inferiority of equipment on the ground, but not in the air. The best pilots in the world using old-generation subsonic fighters can do very little about faster aircraft. Therefore it is vitally important for any country to match its potential rivals' aircraft. The political problem arises because (*a*) only a few countries make jet fighters, (*b*) the planes need a continual flow of spare parts, and (*c*) there is a long 'gestation' period

---

*In fact the post-*coup* military regimes have tended to be even more pro-French than previous civilian regimes.

between the original order and the time when training and ancillary equipment are sufficiently developed for operational use.

Thus, if a country wants to acquire jet fighters it has to be reasonably friendly with one of five countries: Sweden, USA, France, Britain or the USSR.* Once a deal is made, it will need to stay friendly, otherwise the flow of supplementary equipment will stop. Thus the initial purchase is followed by years of dependence. Jet fighters don't 'grow' in economically backward countries where the whole industrial base is lacking, so that the constant up-dating of electronics, air-to-air missiles, radar equipment etc. have to be imported – and from the original source to whose aircraft they are related.

Both sides of the bargain recognize this dependence and the supply of sophisticated weaponry is usually allied with general trade, ideological and political links. At what point is the degree of dependence sufficient to affect the feasibility of the *coup*? Consider the following time-table of relations between the Soviet Union and Egypt from 1955 to 1967:

1955 'Czech' arms deal: this was the first arms supply contract between the Soviet Union† and any Arab state; it was of great political importance for Egypt because it broke the Western arms monopoly‡ and signified 'true' independence.

Effect: the commitment of (future) foreign currency earnings, and the need to keep on friendly terms with the only possible supplier of spare parts.

1956 Suez-Sinai War: the Egyptian defeat in the Sinai resulted in the loss of much equipment; this was quickly replaced by the Soviet Union.

Effect: the commitment to the USSR reinforced and financial indebtedness increased.

*Some other countries manufacture or are in the process of developing jet fighter-type aircraft, including Japan, Italy, Canada and India. But these suppliers are limited either in terms of designs, specifications, resale freedom or production capabilities.

†The arms supply contract was Czech in name only. Kermit Roosevelt of the CIA (State Department) was then Nasir's adviser and he suggested that it should be called 'Czech' to pacify H. Trevelyan, the British Ambassador.

‡Or rather, oligopoly.

1962 Revolution and 'civil war' in the Yemen: after the death of Ahmad Ibn Yahya, ruler of the Yemen, the subsequent revolution and civil war involved Egyptian-supported republicans and Saudi-supported royalists; Egyptian troops were sent to back the Republicans.

Effect: Soviet help needed to keep 30–50,000 troops in the Yemen. Moral and monetary debt increases.

1966 Final break with USA, end of US wheat shipments: the shortfall in food supplies could not be covered by hard currency purchases in the world market.

Effect: Soviet food aid started, making Egypt dependent on the USSR for a significant part of its supplies.

1967 June, Six-Day War, Egyptian defeat in the Sinai. Israeli sources estimated on 20 June that eighty per cent of Egyptian military equipment of all kinds was destroyed or captured.

Effect: as a condition for the re-equipment of Egyptian forces, the USSR required close supervision over army training, the selection of senior military personnel and the organization of intelligence services.

Thus, after twelve years a limited relationship, designed to free Egypt of its dependence on the West for arms supplies, has escalated to a much greater degree of dependence on the USSR: Egypt is now dependent on Soviet goodwill for arms, wheat, and general economic aid. The Soviet navy has shore facilities in Alexandria and Port Said and there are several hundred Russian advisers and instructors in the Egyptian armed forces. Is this enough to allow the Soviet Union to oppose or reverse a *coup*?

The Soviet embassy in Cairo could act as a focus of counter-*coup* activity; it could inspire and deploy the forces of the many Egyptians committed to the Soviet presence; it could certainly regulate appropriately the flow of aid supplies. Even after a *coup*, the USSR could bring about a collapse of the new regime simply by cutting off all aid. Should the regime turn to the USA for help, this will automatically mean that the opponents of the *coup* will be joined by the anti-American element as well. This would at least severely complicate the position of its planners, and in present circumstances it would almost certainly lead to their defeat.

When countries are in such a position of direct and material dependence, the *coup* must be integrated with some immediate post-*coup* foreign policy planning; if the political inspiration of the *coup* is opposed to the greater power, then the *coup* may well fail unless this coloration can be concealed. The few remaining colonies, largely Spanish and Portuguese, are of course formally in a position of total dependence. There, too, as in South Vietnam and East Germany, no *coup* can succeed *in situ* but would have to be carried out in Lisbon or Madrid.

The second pre-condition of the *coup* is therefore:

The target state must be substantially independent and the influence of foreign powers in its internal political life must be relatively limited.

It is a *cliché* that countries are interdependent rather than independent; domestic political issues have international implications, while foreign political developments have domestic repercussions. The commercial, cultural and military ties that link countries give each country a measure of influence in the affairs of the other; even the most powerful nations can be so influenced. Thus, in the period preceding the US intervention in the Second World War, British-influenced and German-influenced political groupings and pressure groups were operating in American domestic politics, just as today the parties in the Middle Eastern conflict exert pressure on the State Department through their respective lobbies.

If even a super-power can be influenced by such weak powers then any definition of independence must be as loose as reality.* Nevertheless some more definite guidelines can be formulated:

(*a*) A *coup* is not worth attempting if a Great Power has significant military forces in the country concerned. If these forces are physically remote from the political centres, and/or if the pre-*coup* regime was moving towards an unfriendly position vis-à-vis the Great Power, the rule does not hold.

*In South Korea, for example, the civil disorders and subsequent *coup* of 1962 do not appear to have been influenced by the significant US military presence in the country.

(b) The *coup* must seek the endorsement of the Great Power if large numbers of its nationals are serving as military or civilian 'advisers'.

The application of these guidelines excludes many otherwise potentially suitable targets: (a) the Spanish, Portuguese and other colonies; (b) East Germany, Hungary, Outer Mongolia, and perhaps Poland; (c) Thailand, Laos, South Vietnam, and (d) some of the African territories still bound by defence agreements with France or the UK subject to the qualifications made above and limited to the smaller countries.

ORGANIC UNITY

In looking at the political consequences of economic backwardness we saw that the crucial element in these was the concentration of all power in the hands of a small *élite*. Conversely, in sophisticated political units power is diffuse and therefore difficult to seize in a *coup*.

We now face another possible obstacle to a *coup*; power may be in the hands of *sectional* forces, who use the government as a 'front', or *regional* forces whose dependence on the supposed political centre is only theoretical.

In both these cases the problem lies in the fact that the seizure of the supposed political centre will not win the battle; the sources of political power may be in other centres which may be too difficult and/or numerous to seize. In both these instances the realities of power are in conflict with the theoretical structure of the state, just as in the cases where the political unit is not truly independent. Here, 'power' is within the country – but not where it is supposed to be; not in this instance because the unit is unsophisticated enough to diffuse power through subsidiary entities, but because the unit is not really *organic*.

Sectional Interests

This is the age of the giant business enterprise. The same factors which have led to the unprecedented prosperity of the modern industrial economy have also systematically favoured the larger business organization; mass production and mass distribution imply large business units. Where the advantages of large-scale production are particularly great, as in the automobile and the chemical industries, *only* the very large enterprise can survive. Elsewhere, where there is no such economic imperative, the giant corporation has developed because of the economies of large-scale marketing, or simply because of the natural dynamics of accumulation. In every industrially developed economy there are such firms: ICI in Britain, General Motors in the United States, Philips in the Netherlands and Fiat in Italy are all firms which have been able to grow sufficiently to emerge from the rest of industry and to become one of its focal points. This position gives them a great deal of economic power because their managerial decisions can affect the entire national economy.

In political terms, however, the power of the giant corporation is just one more element within the business community, and this in turn is just one of the forces competing in the political life of the nation. The corporation may be a giant, but it is a giant amongst many.

It is otherwise in economically underdeveloped countries. If the availability of mineral deposits or of particular crops leads to the development of industry, then because of the nature of these sectors there will be one large firm rather than many small ones. There is by definition little or no other industry; the tax revenues will be small – except for the company's taxes – and there will be very few jobs going, except for the company's jobs. If there are roads and railways, they will have been built by the company as 'company transport facilities'; most of the schools and hospitals will be 'company welfare services'; 'company housing' may dwarf the capital city, and company security guards may be better equipped than the national police.

When the state is poor and fragile the rich and well-organized mining or plantation company will be a great power in the land,* whether it seeks or avoids this power. In fact, it will almost

---

*The material equipment available to the company will, in itself, constitute a considerable source of direct power: its planes, trucks, and telecommunication facilities may well compose a major part of the country's infrastructure.

always be forced to intervene in politics if only to preserve some *status quo*. When the company acts it has a wide range of different weapons it can use, and it can use them at many different levels. The company can slow the flow of tax income to the state by transferring production to some other country in which it operates;* it can boost a particular politician by giving real or sinecure jobs to his supporters; it can buy or bribe the press, and generally exercise the power it derives from being very rich amongst the very poor.

What an industrial empire can do, when set in a backward environment, was illustrated by the Katanga secession in the early 1960s. When Tshombe launched his independent Katanga Republic he had only the meagre resources of a Provincial Governor of the Congolese Republic. Yet as the secession proceeded Tshombe acquired an army with jets, heavy weaponry, armoured cars as well as well-organized propaganda bureaux in London and New York; he was able to recruit (and pay very handsomely) mercenary soldiers and administrators. Katanga has only one major source of wealth: the mining industry owned by the Union Minière, part of the interrelated mining groups which operate in the Copper Belt and South Africa. It does not need a Peking propaganda pamphlet to convince us that Tshombe was financed by the Union Minière – and largely acting as an agent for the company.

But even the Union Minière was operating in what was a relatively unfavourable environment. The Congo is a large country, and there are other mineral deposits worked by other companies with different interests to protect. The typical large-scale enterprise operates in countries where it is the *only* major industry. Thus ARAMCO, the oil company working in Saudi Arabia, is the only major industrial organization in the country. Its 'company town', built to house employees, dwarfs other cities in the area; its taxes constitute almost ninety per cent of government revenue; and it has been responsible for the build-

---

*The risks in the mining and plantation industries are very high and therefore most firms must be very large and they tend to operate in several different countries; they can therefore switch production from one to the other, drastically affecting the countries' finances.

ing of most of the educational, transport and medical facilities in
the country. The Saudi regime has always been efficient at
retaining political control over what was, until recently, a loose
coalition of tribes; the old desert warrior and founder of the
kingdom, Abdul Aziz Ibn Saud, was a past-master at controlling
the tribes and he treated ARAMCO just as another tribe.
Nevertheless, it is clear that ARAMCO is a particularly powerful tribe.

A standard nationalist accusation against the large-scale
foreign enterprise is that it is 'a state within a state', and that it
exercises political power, either through its direct control of the
country's government, or by using the 'leverage' of its home
country on the 'host' country. The United Fruit Company has
often been accused of exercising power through corrupt local
cliques, while the oil companies in the Middle East have been
accused of using both methods.*

A much less plausible accusation against the foreign company
is that it engages in covert activities against the state, such as
sabotage and espionage. Just why it should undertake such
activities is not explained, but such accusations are widely
believed. When the new regime of Husni al-Za'im was set up in
Syria in 1949 one of its first actions was to limit the freedom of
action of the Iraq Petroleum Company. IPC was informed that
(*a*) its aircraft would have to obtain official permits for each
flight; (*b*) that the company's security guards would have to be
replaced by public security forces, and (*c*) that company personnel would need official permits to travel in the border zones.
However unfounded the allegations of complicity in espionage
(which were the supposed reasons for the rules), it should be
noted that such restrictions (except for the last one) are common-
place in most developed countries.

Even if the foreign company has no desire to interfere in the
political life of the 'host' country, it may be forced to do so
merely in order to protect its installations and personnel.
Typically, this is the case when the company is operating in
areas which are not under the effective control of the *de jure*

---

*Joseph Conrad's novel *Nostromo* is a brilliant and prophetic analysis of
the causes and consequences of 'neo-colonialism'.

government, especially in remote areas inhabited by minority groups or – which may amount to the same thing – controlled by local insurgents. The French rubber plantation companies in South Vietnam, for example, have often been accused of financing the Viet Cong. There is no reason to impute sinister motives to them, because since the official government – which also collects taxes – is unable to guarantee law and order, the French plantation companies are simply paying their taxes to the *de facto* government.

The experience of the British oil company in Persia (originally Anglo-Persian, later renamed Anglo-Iranian and finally British Petroleum, before becoming part of the Iranian Oil Consortium), illustrates the case of a business enterprise which was forced to intervene in the domestic affairs of the 'host' country under the pressure of local political realities. Anglo-Persian received its concession from the Persian government in 1901, but it soon discovered that the Tehran government had very little control over the remote areas where the company was actually exploring and later producing oil. The Sheikh of Mohammerah controlled the area at the head of the Persian Gulf, and the neo-Mongolian, Bakhtiari Khans, controlled the rest of Khuzistan; both the Sheikh and the Khans were nominally subject to the Tehran government, but in fact independent.

The company accepted local political realities and in order to protect the safety of its installations entered into arrangements with the local rulers. The British government, however, tried to regularize the situation by supporting the autonomy of the Sheikh against the central government, and the company, being closely associated with the government,* identified itself with the autonomy of the Sheikh. When Reza Pahlavi took power in Persia and restored the authority of the central government the company found itself penalized for its support of the Sheikh.

The relationship between the company and the Bakhtiari Khans was even more complicated. The company realized that its wells and pipelines could only be 'protected' by coming to an arrangement with the local *de facto* power. This time, how-

*The British government bought fifty per cent of the shares of what was to become BP – certainly the best investment of tax-payers' money ever made.

ever, instead of one Sheikh there were many different Khans, all involved in the mutual conflict of tribal politics, with only loose coalitions whose instability prejudiced the security which the company had bought. The 'natural' solution was adopted: the company, together with British consular authorities, entered into tribal politics in order to promote a paramount chief who would clarify and stabilize the situation. The feuds among the Khans, however, were never concluded, and the tribal politics of the company were only brought to an end when the central government of Reza Pahlavi disarmed the Khans and restored its control over the area.

Thus the company, merely in order to protect its installations and to avoid paying double taxation to two rival authorities, had to enter politics at three different levels. It operated in *tribal* politics to promote and maintain the power of the paramount chief of the Bakhtiari; in *national* politics to preserve the autonomy of the Sheikh of Mohammerah against the central government; in *international* politics to 'detach' the Sheikhdom from Persia acting in association with the British consular authorities in the Gulf.

What action must be taken by the planners of the *coup* in the event of the presence of such sub-states in the target country? In a few extreme cases their consent may be necessary: they tend to have their ears to the ground and will probably be aware of the *coup* before the official intelligence outfits. This consent can be obtained by a suitable mixture of threats and promises, and in this case promises do not always have to be kept. Elsewhere they will act as just one more factor with which the *coup* has to deal, but increasingly – after the political education they have received at the hands of nationalist forces everywhere – foreign business interests have learnt that neutrality is sweet.

Regional Entities

The essence of the *coup* is the seizure of power within the main decision-making centre of the state and, through this, the acquisition of control over the nation as a whole.

We have seen that in some cases the decision-making process is too diffused through the entire state bureaucracy and the country at large; in other cases the supposed political centre is controlled by another, foreign centre or by sectional forces which are independent of the whole state machinery.

A similar problem arises where power is in the hands of regional or ethnic *blocs*, who either use the supposed political centre as an agency for their own policies, or ignore the claims of the centre and regard themselves as independent. Practically every Afro-Asian state has border areas, typically mountainous, swampy or otherwise inaccessible, which are inhabited by minority tribes, and where the control exercised by the government is only theoretical. Where this sort of *de facto* autonomy extends to major population centres, the problem of the lack of organic disunity arises; it is, however, of no importance for the *coup* if the organic unit is in itself large – the new regime can deal with local autonomies when it has seized power. Sometimes, however, the local units are so powerful that they control the centre, or else the centre rules only the immediate suburbs of the capital city.

This was often the case in the Congo in the period 1960–64 following Independence and the mutiny of the *Force Publique*. Though the Congolese Republic was constitutionally a unitary, and not a federal, state it quickly lost control of most of the 'provinces', which behaved as totally independent entities. Within each province local factions were in conflict, but the central government's faction tended to be one of the weakest:

Political situation in South Kasai 1960–61

The following groupings were contending for the control of the province:

(*a*) The traditional chiefs. Forces available: tribal warriors.

(*b*) The South Kasai separatists led by 'King' Kalonjii. Forces available: well-equipped, undisciplined troops led by Belgian officers. ('Ex-Belgian' Belgians.)

(*c*) The central government. Forces available: young and inexperienced administrators with loose control over the small national army (ANC) contingent in the eastern part of the province.

(*d*) The Mining company Forminière. Resources available:

financial support and air transport occasionally made available to Kalonjiist and other groups.

The situation in Katanga was even more unfavourable to the central government; the north-east and the Stanleyville area were in the hands of the Gizenga forces; much of the rest of the country could not be reached by government officials because of the breakdown in law and order, and the disruption of transportation facilities. Thus a successful *coup* in Leopoldville (now Kinshasa) would only have won control of a very small fraction of the great Congolese Republic; several different *coups* would have been needed in the various *de facto* capitals, Stanleyville, Elizabethville, Luluaburg, etc. in order to control the whole country.

Federal states represent the overt and constitutional recognition that regions have a local power base and are therefore granted a corresponding measure of local autonomy. In some cases the power of the centre comes from the voluntary union of the regions, and until the central institution develops its own sources of power and authority it is the regions that rule, only using the centre as an agency for their common policies.

The United States was the product of a more or less voluntary union of states and, until the development of Presidential authority in the course of the nineteenth century, the government in Washington was little more than an agency for the common problems of the states. Thus a *coup* staged in Washington in, say, 1800 would have seized an empty symbol, but by 1900 the development of federal authority was such that a *coup* would have led to control over much of the country. The Soviet Union, Canada, India and West Germany are all federal states, but the degree of autonomy of each component state or province varies from the near zero of the USSR to the increasingly independent Canadian provinces. The fact that, constitutionally, Soviet republics are supposed to be fully autonomous (and even entitled to secede from the Federation) is another example of the perpetual contrast between theoretical structures and political realities.

In the event, the realities of power – and of its internal dynamics – tend to lead to a decay of the federal system. The result is either growing centralization (e.g. the USA and USSR) or else growing separation (e.g. India, Canada and pre-*coup* Nigeria).

The idea that political power should be concentrated in one controlling centre for the nation as a whole derives from the presumption that the interests of each region are best served by decision-making in a national framework. This presumption, interestingly enough, is usually accepted only after the destruction of the local power structures. Thus it is agreed by most Englishmen and Frenchmen that major political decisions ought to be made in London and Paris, rather than on a local level. But this intellectual recognition followed, rather than preceded, the crushing of the 'Barons' and of the independent states of Burgundy, Provence, Anjou and Wales.*

In many underdeveloped areas the power of local 'Barons' is still very real, and local movements, based on linguistic or ethnic affiliations, are actively attempting to gain either greater autonomy or else full *de facto* independence. As of January 1968 the central governments of India, Burma, Kenya, Somalia, Ethiopia and Tibet were all experiencing armed conflicts with separatist forces. Canada, India and (as admitted, belatedly, in a grudging footnote) France and the United Kingdom are experiencing political conflicts with separatist elements. In Spain, Yugoslavia and Italy more or less violent separatist groups are operating.

Amongst all these instances, where the local population does not accept the superiority of centralized decision-making, we have to differentiate between the various possible implications for the *coup*:

(a) *The regions are the real centres of power:* the *coup* must either confine itself to one region, or extend to all of them; the supposed centre must be just one more target area. This extends and complicates the *coup*, while the weakness of the *coup*'s forces in each single capital may invite counter-*coup* activity.

(b) *One or two regions dominate the whole country:* this was the

---

*The rise of Celtic separatism in Wales, Scotland, France and Spain has been so rapid and dramatic that perhaps only the absence of jungles is preventing some of their members from starting a home-grown Viet Cong.

situation in pre-*coup* Nigeria. The Northern Region, ruled by traditional Fulani and Hausa emirs, was the largest region by far. Its ruler, the Sardauna of Sokoto (Ahmadu Belloh), was in full control of its internal politics, whereas in the other regions the situation was more fluid – and more democratic. Thus, Ahmadu Belloh, in association with political forces in one other region, dominated the whole Federation. The young Ibo officers, who carried out the first *coup*, therefore had to allocate as much of their efforts to Belloh and his 'capital' as to the federal capital and the federal leadership. In the event, they killed both the federal prime minister (Abubakar Tafawa Balewa) and Belloh. But they were over-extended, so that Ironsi, the senior officer of the army, acting with the police and bureaucracy staged a counter-*coup* and seized power on his own account.

The existence of these regional forces, strong enough to control the supposed centre, may make a *coup* impossible. If the regional or ethnic *bloc* is organized on tribal lines the structures of *its* leadership will be too firm and intimate for a *coup* to function from within. One of the few stable countries of the Middle East, Lebanon, is based on such an arrangement: the Christian, Muslim and Druze *blocs* are all mutually hostile, but they recognize the fact that no single group can hope to dominate all the others. Thus, the Beirut government functions as a common clearing house for those policies which are accepted by each ethnic *bloc*. If one carried out a *coup* in Beirut, it would immediately lead to the collapse of the system, since each group, backed up by their own armed forces, would seize power in their own region. The *coup* would therefore only capture Beirut and its suburbs; and it would probably be unable to retain its control over even that small area.

Lebanon provides an extreme example of the role of ethnic/regional forces. In each individual instance there will be a particular balance of power between the regions, and between the regions and the centre. The efforts of the *coup* would have to be allocated so as to deal with each ethnic or regional bloc on the basis of an estimate of its role in the particular balance of forces. In a few cases a *coup* may be impossible because the nature and extent of regional power is such as to require resources beyond those likely to be available. Elsewhere it will be just one more obstacle to overcome.

The third pre-condition of the *coup* is therefore:

The target state must have a political centre. If there are several centres these must be identifiable and they must be politically, rather than ethnically, structured. If the state is controlled by a non-politically organized unit, the *coup* can only be carried out with its consent or neutrality.

'Ethnically structured' is a rather awkward phrase. It is intended to cover social groups whose leadership is evolved by clear-cut and well-established (usually hereditary) procedures. If a particular traditional leadership controls the state we cannot seize power by carrying out a *coup* in the state's controlling centre, nor can we penetrate the traditional leadership because we would be excluded automatically as usurpers and outsiders. In Burundi, for example, the traditional Watutsi hierarchy controlled the state and therefore to seize power in Burundi it would have been necessary to penetrate the hierarchy, but this would only be possible if (*a*) we were Watutsi, (*b*) we belonged to the aristocracy, and (*c*) we were next in line for the succession. In Rwanda, power was also controlled by traditional Watutsi chiefs who had subjected the Bahutu majority. Then there was a revolution, and now the leadership is Bahutu-political rather than Watutsi-traditional. A *coup* is therefore now possible.

If a political entity is actually controlled by a group which is not structured politically, then obviously political methods cannot be used to seize power. This is the case of a country dominated by a business unit. Imagine, for example, that General Motors *did* control the USA, in the sense that the Presidency and the Congress acted as its stooges. If that were the case, power would have to be seized in Detroit, not Washington. In the unlikely event that one could raise enough cash to buy fifty-one per cent of General Motors' shares, then Washington would be a fringe benefit added to all the other resources controlled. But the *coup* is a *political weapon*, and its planners have only political resources. Thus, GM–USA would be outside the reach – and the scope – of a *coup*.

Returning to reality, Katanga in the early 1960s, and the Central American 'banana' republics of the 1950s were examples of states whose real 'centres' were politically impenetrable – unless you could raise 2–300 million dollars.

3. The Strategy of the *Coup d'État*

'Dean Acheson used to tell a story about Chief Justice Taft relating a conversation he had just had with an eminent man about the "machinery of government". "And you know" – Taft said with wonder in his voice – "he really did believe that it *is* machinery."' *To Move a Nation*, Roger Hilsman

'Under totalitarian conditions knowledge of the labyrinth of transmission belts [of the machinery of government] equals supreme power.' *The Origins of Totalitarianism*, Hannah Arendt

Overthrowing governments is not easy. The government will not only be protected by the professional defences of the state – the armed forces, the police and the security agencies – but it will also be supported by a whole range of *political* forces. In a sophisticated and democratic society these will include political parties, sectional interests, regional, ethnic and religious groupings. Their interaction – and mutual opposition – results in a particular balance of forces which the government in some way represents.* In less sophisticated societies, there may be a narrower range of such forces but there will almost always be some political groups which support the *status quo* and therefore the government.

If those who carry out the *coup* appear to shatter such a powerful structure merely by seizing a few buildings, arresting some political figures and 'liberating' the radio station, it is because their crucial achievement passes unnoticed. This is the dangerous and elaborate process by which the armed forces and the other

*The language of celestial mechanics should not obscure the inevitable distortions which affect the balance of forces.

means of coercion are neutralized, and the political forces temporarily forced into passivity. If we were revolutionaries, wanting to change the structure of society, our aim would be to destroy the power of some of the political forces, and the long and often bloody process of revolutionary attrition can achieve this. Our purpose is, however, quite different: we want to seize power *within* the present system, and we shall only stay in power if we embody some new *status quo* supported by those very forces which a revolution may seek to destroy. Should we want to achieve fundamental social change we can do so after we have become *the* government. This is perhaps a more efficient method (and certainly a less painful one) than that of classic revolution.

Though we will try to avoid all conflict with the 'political' forces, some of them will almost certainly oppose a *coup*. But this opposition will largely subside when we have substituted our new *status quo* for the old one, and can enforce it by our control of the state bureaucracy and security forces. This period of transition, which comes after we have emerged into the open and before we are vested with the authority of the state, is the most critical phase of the *coup*. We shall then be carrying out the dual task of imposing our control on the machinery of state, while at the same time using it to impose our control on the country at large. Any resistance to the *coup* in the one will stimulate further resistance in the other and if a chain reaction develops the *coup* could be defeated.

Our strategy, therefore, must be guided by two principal considerations: the need for maximum speed in the transitional phase, and the need to neutralize fully the forces which could oppose us both before and immediately after the *coup*. If, in the operational phase of the *coup*, we are at any stage delayed, then our essential weakness will emerge: we shall probably acquire a definite political coloration, and this in turn will lead to a concentration of those forces which oppose the tendency we represent (or are thought to represent). As long as the execution of the *coup* is rapid, and we are cloaked in anonymity, no particular political faction will have either a motive, or an opportunity, to oppose us. After all, we could be their potential allies. In any case, a delay will lose us our principal advantage:

the voluntary neutrality of the 'wait and see' elements, and the involuntary neutrality of those forces which need time to concentrate and deploy for action.

The need for maximum speed means that the many separate operations of the *coup* must be carried out almost simultaneously; this in turn requires a large number of people. Therefore, assuming that we start the planning of the *coup* with only a small group of political associates, most of the personnel we will need must be recruited. Further, our recruits must have the training and equipment that will enable them to take swift and determined action. There will usually be only one source of such recruits: the armed forces of the state itself.

It is true that in many countries there are ethnic minorities which, being both traditionally anti-government and warlike, may seem to be ideal recruits for a *coup*. These are typically hill-peoples, like the Druzes of Syria, the Kurds of Iraq, the Shans of Burma and the Pathans of West Pakistan and Afghanistan. Because of their poverty and traditions they would probably be easy to recruit, but to do so may lead to a nationalist reaction on the part of the majority peoples, and since the centres of government are usually located in the majority areas, their opposition would be a further important obstacle to us.

Another possible substitute for the subversion of the forces of the state is the organization of a party militia. When there is a combination of political freedom with an ineffectual maintenance of law and order, such militias are sometimes formed in order to 'protect' party activities. In Weimar Germany, for example, apart from the Brownshirts, there were party militias of the Social Democrats, Communists and the right-wing nationalist parties. Similar organizations – Blackshirts, Greenshirts, Redshirts and, in the Middle East, Silvershirts – spread in many countries in the wake of Fascist and Nazi successes. In spite of their military bearing, their uniforms, and often extensive weaponry, in almost every instance of confrontation between such militias and the forces of the state, the former were defeated.* Thus, when the Nazis tried to use the embryonic

---

*The conflicts between the armed Bolivian tin-miners and army which led to the 1952 revolution are among the very few exceptions.

Brownshirts in the 1923 Munich episode, they were easily overpowered by the police and Hitler was himself arrested. His subsequent rise to power was achieved by *political* means and not by the efforts of the Brownshirts.

In any case, in order to organize and equip a party militia two scarce resources are needed: money and the freedom to do so. Recruiting forces from those maintained by the state requires neither. Therefore, while we will have to neutralize a whole range of forces, a distinctive approach will have to be used in the case of the means of coercion of the state. In dealing with the armed forces, the police and the security services, we will have to subvert some forces while neutralizing the rest; in the case of the political forces the objective will be limited to their neutralization.

Because of their capability for direct intervention, the armed forces and the other means of coercion of the state must be fully neutralized *before* the actual *coup* starts; the 'political' forces can usually be dealt with immediately after the *coup*. In some situations, however, the political forces can also have an immediate impact on the course of events and must, therefore, be treated on the same basis as the means of coercion of the state.

In Russia, during the period of instability which followed the 'bourgeois' February* revolution, the railwaymen's union emerged as a major source of direct power. Vikzhel (the All-Russian Committee of the Union of Railroad Employees) played a decisive role in the defeat of General Kornilov's *putsch* by simply refusing to work the railways carrying his soldiers on their way to Petrograd. Later, when Kerensky fled the city following Lenin's October *coup*, and took refuge with Krasnov's army contingent, Vikzhel threatened to call a general strike (i.e. to leave Krasnov's troops stranded) unless Kerensky negotiated peacefully with the Bolsheviks. Since the Bolsheviks had no serious intention of negotiating, this amounted to a request for unconditional surrender.

In the peculiar conditions of Russia in 1917 the railways, and those who controlled them, were of crucial importance from the

*Old Calendar. Otherwise March and November.

military point of view. Elsewhere there will be other political forces which can exert similar pressures: in poor countries, where the majority of city-dwellers can only buy food on a day-to-day basis, shopkeepers – if well organized – can bring great pressure to bear on the government by refusing to open their shops. Where there is a strong trade-union movement, strikes can impede the vital process of establishing the authority of the new government immediately after the *coup*. Religious and ethnic leaders can use the structures of their communities to organize mass demonstrations against the new regime. We must therefore identify and evaluate these political forces and, if necessary, their leading personalities and co-ordinating bodies must be neutralized before the *coup*.* Other political forces lacking such direct power will also have to be dealt with, but this will be part of the process of conciliation and accommodation which follows the *coup*.

Neutralizing the Defences of the State

One of the outstanding features of modern states is their extensive and diversified security system. This is a consequence of the general breakdown in external security and internal stability which has been experienced in many areas of the world in the last two or three generations. Every state maintains armed forces, a police force and some form of intelligence organization. Many states find it necessary to have paramilitary *'gendarmeries'*, duplicate security services, and other variations on the theme.

In the pre-1914 world, states were not noticeably less aggressive than in present-day international society, but the lack of off-rail transport and a residual attachment to diplomatic convention resulted in a certain time-span between hostility and 'hostilities'. The modern pattern of military operations, the surprise attack and undeclared war, has as a natural consequence the 'military' peace. Instead of small professional armies, acting as cadres for wartime expansion, many states attempt to maintain permanent armies capable of immediate defence – and therefore offence.

*See Chapter 4, in which the neutralization of political forces is discussed.

The rise of ideology-based, revolutionary parties – on both right and left – has led to a similar expansion of internal security forces. 'Political' branches in police forces, para-military internal security forces, under-cover secret police outfits, have all become common features of many states, including 'democratic' ones.

In the 1930s the United States had fewer than 300,000 men in its armed forces; the only significant intelligence operation was a small (and supremely efficient) code-breaking outfit, while internal security forces were limited to a few 'T' men of the Presidential bodyguard and a relatively 'tame' and low budget FBI.

Today, the US Marine Corps alone has more than 280,000 men in uniform while the entire military establishment has a 'population' which at 3,400,000, outnumbers the civilian population of many UN member-countries.

The Intelligence community has developed into a many-headed bureaucratic monster, composed of the CIA, the equally important NSA, the service intelligence outfits, and many defence 'research' institutions. In the internal security field the FBI has tolerated no competitors, except in specialized work, but it has grown into a mini-CIA, with several thousand agents working in the 'political', as opposed to the criminal, function.

No state has been able to emulate such a luxuriant growth, and even the other super-power,* the Soviet Union, has found it impossible to keep up with the USA – in spite of the fact that it gets some of its facilities on the cheap – *à la* Kim Philby. Without being able to keep up with the USA, most states have done their very best. Even a medium-sized country like Italy, with no hostile neighbours of military consequence, with no serious insurgency and with a tame and 'parliamentary' Communist party, has found it necessary to develop an extensive system, comprising two national police forces, several security agencies, a 300,000-man army, a 40,000-man navy and a large air force.

Other more embattled states enroll practically the whole

*The astute editor of *Le Monde* contradicted de Gaulle's assertion that there was only one super-power – the US – by pointing out that there were still two: the United States and the CIA.

population in various kinds of defence and security forces. Israel, surrounded by avowed enemies, with weak natural defences, unprotected by military alliances, is an extreme case: though it only has the population of a medium-sized city it was able to field more than 250,000 men and women in the June 1967 war.

From the point of view of the *coup*, the size and power of the armed forces, police and security agencies is both a great obstacle and a great help. On the one hand, as Trotsky pointed out, the improvement in weapons, transport and communications has widened the gap between organized military forces and civilians equipped with improvised means. Trotsky noted that, while the French mobs of 1789 could 'rush' positions defended by infantry soldiers, in 1917 a Russian mob – however large and determined – would be cut down by 'modern' automatic weapons. By 'modern' he meant the clumsy and slow-firing Maxim machine-gun; today, every single soldier on mob control could be armed with a weapon giving a similar rate of fire.

On the other hand, the increase in the size of uniformed forces and the 'technological revolution' have improved the characteristics of the state security systems as a recruitment ground for the *coup*. The modern army or security force is usually too large to be a coherent social unit bound by traditional loyalties; the need for technically-minded personnel has broken the barriers that often limited recruitment to particular social groups within each country. Pathans and Bedouin may be picturesque and politically very reliable, but they are inadequate as pilots, tank crews, or even to staff a modern police force.

The fact that the personnel of the state security system is both numerous and diverse means that we, the planners of the *coup*, will be able to infiltrate the system. In doing so, we will have the dual task of turning a few of its component units into active participants of the *coup*, while neutralizing the others. This does not mean that we have to fight them, but merely that we have to prevent their possible intervention against us for the limited time-span of the *coup*.

Whether the purpose of our infiltration and subversion of the defences of the state is to turn the unit concerned into an active participant of the *coup*, or whether it is merely defensive, the methods to be followed will depend on the character of each particular organization. The raw material for our efforts is the whole spectrum of the coercive forces of the state, and as these vary substantially in their equipment, deployment and psychological outlook, we shall examine them separately.

NEUTRALIZING THE ARMED FORCES

In June 1967 when the Israelis, having defeated the other Arab armies, were turning to deal with Syria's, the head of Syria's National Revolutionary Council, Salah Jadid, kept the two best brigades of the Syrian army in their barracks at Homs and Damascus.* The War Minister, Hafiz Assad, begged Jadid to be allowed to send the 5th and 70th Brigades to the front, but Jadid – after physically assaulting him – pointed out that, though the brigades might save a few square miles of territory, their use at the front would jeopardize the survival of the regime. The leftist Ba'ath government was not popular with any important section of the population† and the two brigades were the main supports of the regime.

Though hardly patriotic, Jadid was at least realistic. When he had taken power in February 1966, he had done so by means of the two crucial brigades whose officers were politically and ethnically allied to him, and which displaced the previous strong man, Hafez, from power when *his* brigades happened to be away from Damascus – or were infiltrated by Jadid's men.

Everywhere in the world, while the number of doctors, teachers and engineers is only increasing slowly, the numerical strength of armies is expanding very rapidly. It is interesting to note that while technical improvements in, say, agriculture, have allowed a diminishing number of farmers to produce ever larger amounts of food, armies have needed an ever larger 'labour

*R. Atallah, ' *Six jours d'irresponsabilité*', *Jeune Afrique* No. 343, 6 August 1967, pp. 13–15. Also *Der Spiegel*, 23 October 1967.

†Except the small 'Chinese' faction of the Ba'ath party and the Alawite Community.

force' though their productivity – or rather destructivity – per head has also increased very rapidly. A modern platoon of thirty men has about three times the effective fire-power of its 1945 counterpart; it is doubtful whether farming techniques have improved to the same extent.

The effectiveness of modern soldiers, with their rapid transport, reliable communications and efficient weapons, means that even *one* single formation loyal to the regime could intervene and defeat the *coup* if, as is likely, our forces are small and the mass of the people and the rest of the state's forces are neutral. Our investigation of the armed forces of the proposed target state must, therefore, be a complete one: we cannot leave out any force capable of intervention – however small.

Though most states have naval and air forces, as well as armies, we shall concentrate our attention on the latter because the procedures to be followed are usually the same for all three services, and because – with some exceptions – only land forces will be important from the point of view of the *coup*. It is, of course, possible to use fighter-bombers to 'take out' a presidential palace instead of sending a team to arrest the occupant, and this was done in the 1963 Iraqi *coup*, but it is a rather extreme way of playing the game. Although the ratio of fire-power achieved per man subverted is very high indeed, tactical bombing of one's future capital city – and prospective post-*coup* residence – is not calculated to inspire confidence in the new government.

In certain geographical settings, however, the transport element of naval and air forces make them even more important than the army, as for example in the case of Indonesia. With its population centres scattered over several large islands and thousands of small ones, and with the very limited road facilities on the islands, a unit of naval marines – or paratroopers – will be more effective than some much larger army unit located in the wrong place. When the Communist-attempted *coup*-cum-revolution took place in Indonesia the military commanders were able to use their transport potential to great advantage: though Communist-infiltrated army units were very powerful they were in the wrong place; while they sat in the Borneo jungles* the anti-Communist paratroopers and marines took over Jakarta, and the country.

Armies are divided into certain traditional formations, which vary from country to country, such as divisions, brigades, regiments, battalions, companies, platoons. Beyond this theoretical structure, however, the focus of decision-making and the real organizational framework is usually concentrated at one or two particular levels. It is very important for us to identify which level is the important one, and then concentrate our efforts on it. Table 1 illustrates several possible alternatives which we may face, though in order to achieve infiltration in depth we may in fact have to operate on many levels *below* the real centre; operating *above* it would be pointless.

TABLE I. *Formal Structures and Real Chains of Command*

(a) centralized formal structure	real chain of command
GHQ	GHQ
army area HQ	
division	
brigade	
battalion	battalion
company	company
platoon	platoon

(b) de-centralized formal structure	real chain of command
GHQ	GHQ
army area HQ	army area HQ
division	division
brigade	brigade
battalion	
company	company
platoon	platoon

*It is ironic that ex-President-for-life Sukarno sent them there in order to oppose the Malaysian Federation in the 'confrontation' which the new government eventually liquidated.

(c) *modern NATO-style structure* formal structure	*real chain of command*
GHQ army area HQ division brigade battalion company platoon	GHQ army area HQ brigade company platoon

In (a) in the table, the operational echelon is the battalion; if there are persons holding the rank of divisional commanders they will probably be officers who have been eliminated from the real chain of command, and given gaudy uniforms and exalted ranks as a sweetener. If, in this case, we were to subvert a brigade or divisional commander, and he then issued orders on our behalf to the battalion, the latter – used as it is to receiving its orders direct from GHQ – will probably query or report the order. Thus apart from mere ineffectiveness there could also be a further risk in operating at the wrong echelon.

In (b) where almost every echelon is operational, we can subvert the control mechanism at almost any level and orders given on our behalf will be obeyed at each lower level. In (c) again we can operate at all levels except those of division and battalion.

Though it may seem that the location of the main focus of control and communications is an arbitrary one, in reality it depends on very firm psychological and technical factors. Unless the standard of training and motivation is high enough, men have to be welded into great uniform *blocs* under the firm control of their superiors, because they have neither the discipline nor the capability to fight as individuals. Even highly-motivated soldiers cannot be allowed to operate far from the concentration of troops unless they are linked by an efficient system of communications which enables them to receive new orders and to report on their situations. In general, the easier the terrain, the lower the degree of discipline and efficiency, the larger will be the unit allowed to operate independently. Conversely, the more sophisticated the troops and equipment, and the closer the terrain – as in jungles or swamps – the smaller will be the unit operating on its own.

The two extremes came face to face in the Sinai in the 1967 Arab–Israel war when the Egyptian army was organized into three large *blocs* under rigid HQ control and incapable of independent action; the Israelis, on the other hand, operated in many small brigade-sized groups which concentrated for mass, and separated to infiltrate in a fluid and flexible manner.

When we have determined which is the true operational echelon in the various formations of the country concerned, we can go on to the next stage: identifying which formations have the capability to intervene – for or against the *coup*. We shall follow two main criteria: the nature of the unit concerned, and the location of the particular unit. These are explored in a case study of the Portuguese armed forces.

The Portuguese Armed Forces: Situation 1967

The present regime in Portugal can fairly be described as a partnership between the land-owning classes, the newly-emergent industrial and business interests, and the bureaucratic middle class (this staffs the civil service and the officer-level of the armed forces). As in Spain, the air force and navy are staffed by elements which are traditionally less conservative than the army officers; as in Spain, the two services have been kept 'thin' in numbers and resources.

ARMY: The total strength is about 120,000 men, distributed as follows (excluding administrative personnel):

1 infantry division, with some medium tanks, which is partially used as a training formation and is at about one half of its theoretical establishment. Of the total number of men in the unit, only about 2,000 have any transport, apart from the small number equipped with armour. At any one time many of the troops will be newly conscripted, with little training or discipline.

Location: central Portugal.

1 infantry division: this formation is usually much below strength, with perhaps 3,000 men with some degree of training. Transport is sufficient for perhaps half this number.

Location: northern Portugal.

Rest of the army: the largest number of troops, around 100,000, with the highest degree of training and with the best equipment, is spread over the African territories: Angola, Mozambique and Guinea.

NAVY: Though the Portuguese have a great naval tradition, and though the overseas 'provinces' would justify a larger navy (which the US military assistance programme could have partially paid for), for the reasons suggested above it has been kept relatively weak: one destroyer, fourteen smaller combat ships, three submarines and thirty-six other vessels. Of greater interest to us: twelve support ships, four landing-craft, and half a battalion of marines. Because of the distance of the African provinces, even if the navy were particularly loyal to the regime, it could not rapidly bring over many troops from there. The marines tend to be in distant waters and, in any case, their number is hardly significant.

AIR FORCE: About 14,000 men. It is equipped with a variety of old American and Italian equipment. Its 3,000 paratroopers are stationed in the African provinces, while the transport wing would be able to carry back to Portugal only about a thousand men every twenty-four hours.

In the case of Portugal, therefore, though the armed forces number about 150,000 men, only a small fraction of this total would be relevant in the event of a *coup.* Most of them would be prevented from intervening physically in the Lisbon area because of their location and their lack of suitable transport equipment. Others would only be able to intervene ineffectually, since their training and equipment would be unsuitable. Thus, out of the entire armed forces, only three or four battalions (perhaps 4,000 men) would have an effective intervention capability. The small size of this force reduces the possibility of the *coup* being defeated, but it also limits our potential area of recruitment.

If the Air Force or the Navy did bring back to Portugal some of the troops stationed in Africa, by the time of their arrival *we* would be the government, and they would therefore be under our orders. If we should fail to impose our authority by then, the *coup* would have failed anyway and their arrival would not change matters. Unless, that is, we had subverted the troops in Africa, which would be a rather tortuous way of going about things.

This suggests the principal criteria by which we separate out the forces relevant to the *coup*, whether military or not:

The forces relevant to a *coup* are those whose locations and/or equipment enables them to intervene in its locale (usually the capital city) within the 12–24-hour time-span which precedes the establishment of its control over the machinery of government.

Infiltrating the Armed Forces

Our initial survey of the armed forces of the target country will have isolated two items of information which are crucial to the planning of the *coup*. These are, the nature and composition of the units which have an intervention capability, and the real operational echelon within them. This data is illustrated in the notional table below:

TABLE 2. *Country X: Potential Forces of Intervention*

(a) *battalion-size force*

   1,000 men, organized in 10 companies, with mechanical transport and anti-tank weapons.
   Location: capital city. Operational echelon: battalion HQ.

(b) *division-size force*

   1,500 men, organized in 20 companies, with armoured carriers, 25 tanks.
   Location: 30 kilometres from capital city. Operational echelon: brigade HQ; tanks under separate battalion HQ.

(c) *brigade-size force*
   3,000 men, organized in 3 battalions.
   Location: 300 kilometres from capital city; air transport available.
   Operational echelons: brigade HQ and air force squadron HQ.

Hitherto we have been thinking in terms of formal military units, but we must now carry our analysis further in order to identify the 'key' individuals within each particular unit. If we were dealing with a primitive military organization we could readily isolate those who effectively lead the unit concerned. In the tribal-war-band, for example, there will be a few obvious 'leader' types, distinguished by their appearance and less obviously by their descent or personal repute; the other warriors will only be functionally different from each other because of their individual strength or dexterity. In modern military organizations it is otherwise: the efficiency of the organization depends on the use of many different types of weapons and other facilities, handled by specialized personnel. In each situation there will be an appropriate 'mix' of these and the system therefore depends on two kinds of 'key' individuals: the 'technicians' and those who co-ordinate them, the 'leaders'.*

Our next problem, therefore, is to determine who are the 'key' individuals within those units of the armed forces which could intervene – for or against us – during the *coup*. As we have already determined which is the 'operational' echelon within each particular formation and thus implicitly identified the 'leaders', we now turn to the identification of the technicians. Who these are will depend on the nature of the organization and the task to be carried out. If, for example, during the course of the *coup* the government calls on the help of force (c) in our notional Table 2, its arrival in the capital could be prevented with the cooperation of just one of these groups:

   (i) the staff operating the communication system between the political leadership and force (c);
   (ii) the pilots and/or ground-staff of the air transport squadron;

*The 'leaders' will usually be the operational officers of the unit concerned, but this need not always be so. See footnote on page 73.

(iii) the guard force at the airport/s;

(iv) the control-tower personnel at either airport, especially in difficult flying conditions.

In general, the more sophisticated the organization, the greater is its efficiency – but also its vulnerability. Either force (*a*) or force (*b*) in Table 2 could for example, operate successfully even if quite a few of its personnel were not cooperating with the leadership. For these forces, losing the cooperation of ten per cent of their men would mean losing approximately ten per cent of their effectiveness; in the case of force (*c*), however, the loss of perhaps one per cent of its men could lead to a *total* loss of effectiveness for some particular tasks (such as intervening in the capital city).

This indicates that insofar as we are trying to neutralize a formation of the armed forces, we should do so through the cooperation of *technicians* rather than *leaders*, because the former are both more effective individually and easier (and safer) to recruit. The second rule is that we should, other things being equal, choose for neutralization those units which have the most complex organization, while choosing the simplest ones for incorporation. This will both reduce *our* vulnerability from a sudden defection and minimize the total number of people that must be ultimately recruited.

Before we go on to approach and persuade the 'key' individuals to join us (thus giving us effective control of their units) we must have collected sufficient information on the armed forces to know:

(*a*) which are the military units which could intervene at the time and place of the *coup*;

(*b*) the real command structure within the relevant units, and who are the leaders;

(*c*) the technical structure of the units and who are the technicians.

To 'incorporate' a unit we will need the active cooperation of a number of its leaders, and in the case of a technically simple unit the defection of some technicians will not matter greatly. If, in otherwise well-infiltrated units, some of the leaders should remain loyal to the pre-*coup* regime, this should not prove to be a major obstacle.*

Whether we concentrate on leaders or on technicians will depend on the particular structure of the effective forces of intervention and on the particular political climate. If there is a sharp political division between the troops and their officers we may be able to incorporate units without the cooperation of any formal leaders at all. The problem of identifying the unofficial leaders will, however, be a very difficult one, and in any case there is no reason to believe that we are planning the *coup* at a time when such a division has hardened. The technical structures however, are more stable, and one of our principal considerations will be to avoid being dependent on too many links of the technical chain. Table 3 (p. 74) shows our optimum strategy in infiltrating a typical set of potential intervention forces.

Of course, in countries prone to *coups*, those who order these things are aware of their vulnerability to the defection of parts of their armed forces. It is therefore quite likely that the 'easy' battalion No. 1 has been carefully chosen for its reliability and its commanders are trusted associates of the ruling group. If this is the case, we may have to work on battalion No. 3. What we must *not* do is to rely on battalion No. 2, because the defection from our cause of even a few of its 'technicians' would have dramatic consequences.

Until we actually start to collect information about the individuals and to make the first approaches, we may not know which units are politically 'tied' to the regime, and more generally we will not know what are our ultimate recruitment prospects in each unit. Therefore, though we will have a rough classification in mind, dividing the units into potential allies and potential neutrals, we should keep the distinction flexible. As we build up a picture of the recruitment potential in each unit, we will concentrate our efforts on the units to be incorporated; the reliability of a unit 'allied' to the *coup* will be increased if we

*Officers are amazingly expendable. In both France and Russia many officers left their units following the respective revolutions, and yet the armies seemed to experience a sudden increase in their efficiency. Certainly the French military record after 1789 was a great improvement on the preceding thirty years, and so was the Russian after 1917.

TABLE 3. *Optimum Infiltration Strategy*

Unit:	Battalion No. 1	Battalion No. 2	Battalion No. 3
Command	10 company commanders and 5 effective 'leaders' at the HQ of each battalion. For infiltration in depth 30 platoon commanders may have to be subverted in each battalion.		
Key men: Technical Structure:	15-45 'leaders' Very simple. Relies on ordinary communication and transportation equipment.	15-45 'leaders' Very complex. To bring the force to the scene of the *coup*, airlift and sophisticated communications are required.	15-45 'leaders' Medium. Relies on land transport, but radio links needed to operate communications.
Key men: Optimum Strategy:	No 'technicians' Bring a proportion of the 'leaders' over to the *coup* (unit incorporated).	40 'technicians' Secure the passive cooperation of some of the 'technicians' (unit neutralized).	5 'technicians' If battalion No. 1 proves difficult to infiltrate, this one would be the second choice.

infiltrate it in depth, but there is little point in over-infiltrating a unit which will eventually be neutralized. Every approach to an individual will involve an element of risk; every increase in the number of those who know that something is up, will reduce our overall security level. We must therefore avoid over-recruitment.

If we go up to an army officer and ask him to join in a pro-jected *coup*, he will be faced – unless he is a total loyalist – with a set of options, offering both dangers and opportunities.

The proposition could be a 'plant' of the security authorities to determine his loyalty to the regime. The proposition could be genuine, but part of an insecure and inefficient plot, and, finally, the proposition could come from a team that has every chance of success.

Should the proposal be a 'plant', accepting it could lose him his job and much more, while reporting it would gain him the rewards of loyalty. Should it be a genuine proposal he has the uncertain prospect of benefiting after a *coup*, as against the certain prospect of benefiting immediately from reporting it. The natural thing for him to do, therefore, is to report it.

The whole technique of the approach is designed to defeat this logic. Apart from the rewards of being part of a successful *coup* (which can be portrayed as being significantly greater than the rewards of loyalty) there is another factor which operates in our favour. This is that the person to whom an approach is reported may himself be a supporter of the *coup*. We must therefore emphasize these two points as much as possible, while underplaying the risk element. But, hopefully, our potential recruits will be motivated by some considerations beyond greed and fear, with other interests and affiliations entering their choice: links of friendship with the planners of the *coup*, and a shared political outlook will be important, but usually the crucial considerations will be family, clan and ethnic links with those planning the *coup*.

In most economically backward countries the different ethnic groups are only imperfectly fused into one entity and mass education and mass communications have not by any means broken down traditional rivalries and suspicions. In any case, the first steps towards economic progress usually reinforce these conflicts, and we may often find that ethnic links are far more important than more recent political affiliations.

For example, when no steel mills were being built there could be no regional conflicts on where to build them; when civil-service jobs were all given to citizens of the imperial power there could be little conflict between ethnic groups on the 'fair' allocation of jobs. Conflicts over jobs or the location of steel mills are necessarily more intense than the old conflicts over land: while before, only the geographical fringes of the tribe were in contact with the rival, now each tribe fights the other on the national stage. While a conflict over land can reach a compromise at some middle line, a steel mill has to be located in either area A or area B. (The alternative, of course, is to put it on the border of the two provinces; although this is usually far from roads and other facilities, it is sometimes done.)*

As old conflicts widen in scope and intensity, the instinctual solidarity of the ethnic groups hardens. African 'tribalism' is merely an extreme case of a very general phenomenon – for example, sophisticated and utterly unreligious Jews will 'happen' to marry other Jews, though they may regard themselves as thoroughly assimilated. Despite Czech and Slovak protestations of national unity, capital investment has had to be assigned carefully to each area on an exact percentage basis, and conflict over this was one of the factors which brought down the Novotny ('the great survivalist') government in 1968. In fact, all over Eastern Europe the old conflicts are just below the surface, and the new 'socialist-national' policies are inevitably reviving them.†
In Rumania almost half a million Germans and a million and a half Hungarians feel that they are not getting a fair deal; while in Yugoslavia, Croats, Serbs, Dalmatians and Macedonians are all involved in the ethnic balancing act, not to speak of the smaller Albanian, Vlach and Slovene groups. In many areas, ethnic divisions are complicated by a superimposed religious conflict. The Ibo nation in Nigeria, for example, has been in endemic conflict with the Muslim northerners for a very long time, but the introduction of Christianity among them has meant that the old Ibo/Hausa conflict has been intensified by a new Muslim/Christian one.

We will therefore make the fullest use of the 'ethnic matrix' without, however, aligning our *coup* with any particular ethnic faction. In terms of petty tactics, we will match each potential recruit with a recruiter who shares his affiliation and, if necessary, the image of the *coup* will be presented in a similar vein.

---

*The problem is compounded by the fact that development programmes are usually focused around one or two big projects, which attracts much of the country's attention – and investment funds. The 'donor' countries usually resist the fragmentation of industrial projects to appease local feelings and this further complicates the political problem.

†The 'Zionist plot' in Poland in early 1968 and the perpetual conflict between Hungary and Rumania over the Transylvanian provinces are particular examples of a general problem.

But we must also take account of a special factor which is a typical post-colonial phenomenon. Colonial regimes developed the habit of recruiting army personnel among minority ethnic groups, which were reputed to be more warlike and, more important, could be trusted to join in the repression of the majority group with enthusiasm. After independence, these minorities naturally regressed in terms of political power and social position, but they still staffed much of the armed forces. This has led to the strange spectacle of minorities acting as the official protectors of the regime which is putting the pressure on them.

The Druzes and Alawites of Syria have been in this position since the French departed in 1945, and it is hardly surprising that disaffected officers of the two groups have played a prominent role in most of the many *coups* since independence.

In many parts of Africa the majority peoples are the reputedly 'soft' coastal tribes,* who have captured the political leadership because of superior numbers and education, while much of the army is made up of members of the smaller hill-tribes. This is the result of the superficial ethnographic theory that the British learnt in India and the French in Algeria, but which, in African conditions, was little less than absurd. As soon as the officers of the colonial country landed in a new territory, they set about finding the hills and, once there, tried to recreate their semi-homosexualizing relationship with the 'wily Pathan' or *'le fier Kabyle'*, by recruiting the supposedly 'tough' hill-men into the army.

Without setting the stage for an inter-tribal civil war, there is every incentive to make use of this factor but, to the extent that there is an effective political life, the ideological outlook of the potential recruit will also be important. As far as we are concerned, combining all ranges of the political spectrum against a right or left extreme will give the most suitable political 'cover' to our *coup*. The Qassem regime in Iraq, which lasted for five years as a pure balancing act, was finally brought down in 1963

*Nigeria is the exception, where the coastal nations are much more developed but fewer in numbers than the inland Hausas, and that is the cause of the trouble.

TABLE 4. *The Role of Ethnic Minorities in Syrian Politics*

The Druzes

1949, April:
The first post-colonial regime of President Quwatli tries (and fails) to destroy the power base of a major Druze clan. This was one of the factors which led to the pioneering *coup* of Husni al-Za'im (the first military dictator in the Arab world).

1949, August:
Husni al-Za'im overthrown by a group of officers, of whom many are Druzes; this followed the attempt to intimidate the Druze *Jabal* area. The crucial armoured-unit commanders were Druzes whose co-operation had been enlisted by the planners of the *coup*.

1949, December:
The new regime starts its attempt to unite Syria with Iraq, and a new *coup* is planned to overthrow it and stop the union. Druze officers of the armoured unit carry out the *coup*, which leads to Shishakli's military dictatorship.

1954, February:
Shishakli's regime overthrown. This was preceded by his military occupation of the *Jabal Druze* area and his arrest of a Druze delegation, which led to disturbances and reprisals. The group which carried out the *coup* was composed of three factions, of which the *Druze* was perhaps the most important.

The Alawites

1966, February:
Coup by the leftist Ba'ath against the rightist Ba'ath regime of Hafiz and the party founders, M. Aflak and S. Bitar. The *coup* was supposedly based on an ideological rift within the Ba'ath movement. In fact, the government of the leftist Ba'ath was a cover for a group of Alawite officers headed by Salah Jadid, himself an Alawite.

1967, February:
The Chief of Staff, a Sunni Muslim, is replaced by an Alawite; political power retained by the Alawite-controlled National Revolutionary Council, with Sunni and Christian Arab ministers as figureheads.

---

when the moderate nationalist, Aref (Abdel Salam), persuaded all political factions, from left-wing Ba'ath to right-wing conservatives, to combine against the supposed Communist penetration in the government.*

If there is no extreme faction available, however, we will have to be content with the petty tactics of claiming political kinship with potential recruits. But apart from the virtues of honesty there is a need for consistency and a systematic presentation of the *coup* in terms of divergent political 'lines' may eventually lead to our undoing.

Finding out the ethnic group to which a particular officer belongs is relatively easy; finding out what is his political outlook is rather more difficult. But the hardest thing of all will be to find out if he is personally alienated from the higher military leadership. Only the family and the closest friends of an officer will know whether he feels that his superiors are treating him unfairly, or running things badly, to the extent that he would welcome a radical change in the whole set-up. Unless we have a direct line to the individual concerned, we will have to use outside information to determine his inner feelings.

A standard intelligence procedure is to follow the career pattern of officers, in order to find out which ones have been passed over for promotions, assuming – other things being equal – that they will make good prospects for recruitment. In many countries, promotions within the armed forces are announced in official gazettes, and starting from a particular class at the military academy, one can follow the career of each officer from their graduation to the present. In some countries, where promotions are not published (for security reasons), one can carry out the exercise by using back-copies of the telephone directory where their names will be printed along with their changing ranks. Where, as in the Soviet Union, neither telephone directories nor official gazettes are good sources of information, we could use more desperate expedients: getting an old boy from

---

*One of the danger signs was the fact that Qassem started calling his opponents 'fascist Hitlerites'. Adolf Hitler is a popular figure with most shades of Arab opinion and only an unthinking transposition of Soviet habits could have led to the use of this epithet.

the relevant years to circulate proposals for a reunion, or building up mini-biographies from personal acquaintances; by whatever means, our aim would be to trace a reasonably accurate
career history for each graduating class from the military
academy. The competitive position of each officer will be
established *vis-à-vis* others of his year, rather than the other
officers of the formation in which he serves, and Table 5 presents the information in the appropriate framework:

TABLE 5. *Class of 19 – Military Academy of Country X:*
       Present Career Position

lieutenant	7
captain	55
major	33
colonel	18
brigadier	2
deceased or civilian	15
	130

The seven lieutenants will probably make eager recruits for
anything that will disturb – and rearrange – the order, but their
low rank may be a correct assessment of their abilities, in which
case their 'help' may be a liability. More generally, and more
usefully, we will know that the captains and majors in our table
may well be less enthusiastic about the set-up than the colonels,*
while the two brigadiers – if not actually appointed for their
political reliability – have probably become staunch supporters
of whoever gave them their exalted jobs.

Ethnic affiliation, political outlook, and career patterns will all
serve as guides to the likely reaction of the potential recruit when
the approach is made. There are, however, two points that we
have to bear in mind, the first organizational, and the second

*Of course, colonels have always been prominent in military *coups*, but
these have been *coups* which they have initiated on their own behalf. Our
purpose is to *use* army officers, and captains are less likely to take the *coup*
out of our hands than more senior officers.

deeply human. While alienated personnel will make good recruits, we must remember that we need people who will not only cooperate personally, as in the case of the technicians, but also bring the units they command over to the *coup*. Thus, while the leaders we recruit could (and should) be estranged from the superior hierarchy, they must not be 'outsider' figures who are not trusted by their fellow-officers and men. There will often be a danger of attracting the inefficient, the unpopular, the corrupt, as well as the disaffected. If we allow our *coup* to be assisted by such men we will be endangering the security of the *coup* and discouraging the recruitment of the better elements, and – most important of all – we may find that our 'leader' recruits will fail to bring their units with them.

The other point to bear in mind is the basic unpredictability of human behaviour. We have so far been trying to establish which links could override the loyalty of army personnel to their superiors and, of these affiliations, the strongest may be expected to be a family link. We should not, however, place total reliance on this factor. Although there is an Arab proverb: 'I and my brother against my cousin; I and my cousin against the world', we should remember the Aref family history in Iraq between 1958 and 1968 (Table 6).

The relationship between the brothers illustrates the difficulty of predicting human behaviour. Between 1958 and 1962 one brother was in prison under a suspended death sentence, while the other was in charge of a force that could probably have moved on the capital at any time. The Ba'ath leaders, mindful of this precedent, allowed Abd-el-Rahman to remain in charge of the important armoured units near Baghdad, and this was their undoing. There was a period, immediately after the first *coup* of 1963, when the position of the Presidential brother was weak and the Ba'ath party militia, totally untrained but heavily armed, could have been used to remove the military brother from his command. The Ba'ath leaders, however, assumed that Abd-el-Rahman would not collaborate with his brother and would behave as he did in 1958 and 1959–62. This time he behaved differently, in spite of the fact that he was helping a brother who needed help much less badly than in 1958–62, when he was a

TABLE 6. *The Aref Brothers in Iraq, 1958–68: A Study in Loyalty*

The recent ruler of Iraq, President Abd-el-Rahman Aref,* was chosen as a compromise candidate by the army after the accidental death of his brother, Abd-el-Salam, the previous dictator of Iraq in April 1966. The career pattern of the two brothers shows that, while both were prominent army leaders, one did not always cooperate with the other:

	Abd-el-Salam	*Abd-el-Rahman*
July 1958: *Coup* overthrows the monarchy.	Co-author of the *coup* with Qassem.	Unaware of the plans and only intervenes at the end – though commander of an important armoured unit.
November 1958:	Qassem arrests Abd-el-Salam. Accused of treason and given a (remitted) death sentence.	Promoted, and placed in charge of a large army contingent.
1962:		Placed in retirement.
February 1963: Ba'ath *coup*. Qassem deposed and shot.	Released and made President.	Placed in charge of the 5th armoured division, promoted to brigadier-general.
November 1963: Anti-Ba'ath *coup*.	Planned by brothers together.	
	Assumes full control.	Promoted.
April 1966:	Dies.	Emerges as compromise Presidential candidate of the army.

captive and under a death sentence (or perhaps because of this).

Despite such instances of human unpredictability, and bearing in mind the individuality of our prospective recruits we can nevertheless use the information we have collected to rank the leaders in terms of their probable response.

Having established the career histories and ethnic and political affiliations of possible recruits, we can proceed to weigh our

*Abd-el-Rahman Aref has since been overthrown by a *coup d'état*.

prospects as illustrated in Table 7. In evaluating the information we must, of course, bear in mind that the importance to be attached to each factor will differ from one environment to

TABLE 7. *Battalion No. 1: Recruitment Prospects, see Table 3 (p. 74)*

Recruitment prospects of fifteen officers of higher rank. Experience, opinions and affiliations from the point of view of the *coup*. (Repeat for thirty platoon commanders.)

x = favourable   n = unfavourable   o = unknown
xx = very favourable   nn = very unfavourable

Officer No.	Political Views	Ethnic affiliations	Career pattern	Approach Yes	Approach No	Approach Doubtful
1	o	x	xx	√		
2	n	xx	n		√	
3	xx	xx	xx	√		
4	nn	x	n		√	
5	nn	nn	nn		√	
6	x	x	x	√		
7	o	xx	nn			√
8	o	n	xx	√		
9	n	xx	n		√	
10	o	nn	xx	√		
11	x	n	o			√
12	x	x	x	√		
13	n	n	n		√	
14	xx	xx	x	√		
15	o	n	xx	√		

another: in Latin America, for example, social background would also have to be added, while in Western Europe and North America political allegiance would be paramount – ethnic affiliation would be of little importance, but social background would carry some weight.

Thus, out of fifteen potential recruits we see that No. 3 is the only totally good prospect from the point of view of the factors here taken into consideration; No. 5 is a totally bad one, and probably dangerous to approach at all; the others, however, will be somewhere in the middle.

Once we have repeated the procedure followed in the case of battalion No. 1 and we have covered all the other formations of the armed forces (or at any rate those with an effective intervention capability), we will know the overall recruitment prospects of each unit, and within them, of each individual. We will never be able to achieve a 100 per cent coverage; in some cases, where the armed forces are very large in relation to our resources, or frequently redeployed, our coverage may be very incomplete.

This will not matter greatly if the 'unknown' units can be neutralized *technically*. If, however, their intervention capability does not depend on elaborate and vulnerable facilities, then the *coup* may be jeopardized. We do not, however, depend on the incorporation and the neutralization procedures alone, and we will also be able to isolate physically those units which appear on the scene unexpectedly and those which we have not been able to infiltrate at all. Before looking at the problems involved in the third, and least desirable, of our methods of dealing with armed opposition, we must turn our attention to the subversion of individuals in the units where we *do* have the requisite information.

As soon as we emerge from the close security of the planning and information stage, the danger factor in our activities will increase very sharply. As we have pointed out earlier, every single individual we approach will be a potential informer who by telling the authorities about our efforts could lead to the collapse of the *coup*. The most dangerous person to approach will be the first in each particular formation, because until we have *his* cooperation we will not have a really intimate source of information about the unit and its members. Our first recruit must, therefore, be a long-standing member of that particular formation and, if at all possible, he must be a senior officer – or even the commander. Once we have chosen our man, the first step will be to arrange a meeting and to 'sound' him out in vague and generalized terms about the 'possibilities of achieving political reform'. These soundings must be conducted by a man, or men, who fulfils certain exacting qualifications: he or she must be a trusted associate of high calibre without, however, being in the inner group planning the *coup*. In other words he must be both valuable and expendable. This is an ideal which we can only try to approximate, but it could be fatal to expose a member of the inner group to the possibility of being betrayed to the authorities. In the *coup* country *par excellence*, Syria, political leaders have in fact gone round the barracks 'canvassing' for (armed) support, but the special conditions of Syrian political life are not likely to be reproduced elsewhere.

Once the potential recruit has been brought to the state when the possibility of a *coup* has been openly discussed, he should be told three things about the *coup*: (*a*) the political aim; (*b*) that we have already 'recruited' other individuals and units and (*c*) the nature of the task that he will be asked to perform. Everything we say, or arrange to be said, to the potential recruit will have to be studied carefully, and we will work on the assumption that every recruit may be a 'double' working for the security services.

We will not, of course, identify our *coup* with any particular party (whose policies would be known) nor with any political faction (whose leading personalities will be known). We will, instead, state the aim of the *coup* in terms of a political attitude rather than in terms of policies or personalities, because the latter are necessarily more specific and therefore liable to specific opposition. The attitude which we will project will have to be calculated carefully: it should reflect the pre-occupations of the target country, implying a solution to the problems which are felt to exist, and in *form* it must reflect the general political beliefs of the majority of its people. Thus, in Britain, we could speak of 'the need for more business-like government' – one can even imply (whether truthfully or not) that the *coup* is linked with prominent public figures such as newspaper proprietors, big-business men or the chairman of a nationalized industry. In Latin America the attitude presented may, for example, imply that the 'sacred trust of the armed forces' requires intervention to 'clear the mess made by the politicians' in order to achieve 'social/national progress, while respecting property rights/individual rights'.

If the pre-*coup* government is itself the product of a seizure of power, then the aims of the *coup* can be presented purely in terms of restoring 'normal political life', or, if we are *outré* leftists we can speak about 'the need to restore Democracy'.

Making up slogans may seem to be an easy game, but in fact our slogans will have to be calculated carefully to satisfy a political optimum. We must, for example, avoid being specific, but if the attitude we present is too general it will stimulate the suspicions of the shrewder of our listeners, while failing to fire the enthusiasm of the more idealistic ones. We must also remember that the armed forces of many countries are often politically, and psychologically, out of tune with civilian society, and that they could have distinct – and perhaps antagonistic – preoccupations and beliefs. As citizens, army officers may share the belief that there ought to be economies in government expenditure, but at the same time feel that the armed forces are being starved of funds. Where the social status of military personnel has suffered a decline because of defeat in battle, or just a long peace, we will always emphasize the need 'to restore the defenders of society to their proper place within it . . .'

In presenting the aims of the *coup* to potential recruits we should exercise a measure of flexibility in order to reach a 'good fit' with what we know to be their beliefs: we cannot, however, run the risk of being exposed as being grossly inconsistent. Whether we hold the views that will make up our image does not matter at all as long as the other conditions are satisfied. It is, incidentally, polite to indicate that the *coup* is only being carried out with extreme reluctance, and that we appreciate that this reluctance is shared by our recruit.

Once the idea of the *coup* has gained a measure of acceptance in the mind of our potential recruit, we should define the *coup* in terms of his role within it. This will not imply that we will reveal any of the operational detail, but we should make it quite clear that:

(*a*) his role will be limited to a few specific actions;
(*b*) almost everybody in his unit is already with us, and
(*c*) therefore his role will be a safe one.

When, and only when, the recruit becomes actual, rather than potential, we can reveal to him the nature of his actual task. This will be described in the greatest possible detail, but not so as to enable the recruit to work out the implications of the task he is asked to perform. If, for example, the recruit in question is destined to use his unit to provide 'muscle' for a roadblock team, he will be told what equipment his men should have, how many will be required and how he will receive the go-signal. He will not be told the date of the *coup*, the place where the roadblock will be, or what the other teams will be doing.

Information is the greatest asset we have, and much of our advantage in the planning stage will derive from the fact that, while we know a great deal about the defences of the state, those who control them know very little about us. We must therefore make every effort to avoid giving any information beyond what is actually required. In any case, while a recruit may feel that he ought to know more about the *coup* before he agrees to participate in it, he will also feel more secure if we show concretely that the operation is being run with great caution, and is therefore secure.

After the first few recruits in each unit have been made, the others in it will be much easier to persuade; there will also be more people to do the persuading, because this is the purpose to which we will put our first recruits, in the interval between their initial recruitment and the actual *coup*. Also, a 'snowball' or, hopefully, an 'avalanche' effect will be generated by the first recruits, who will gradually create a climate in which it will be easy to recruit further.

After the approach and persuasion of the 'key' individuals has begun to give its results, we will be able to identify the units which will eventually be used as active participants in the *coup*. These will be a small part of the armed forces as a whole but hopefully, the *only* part that will be able to play an active role at the time and place of the *coup*. We will concentrate our further efforts on them because their infiltration in depth will be of value to us, whereas the 'over-neutralization' of the other forces will merely involve further risk. Ideally, we will have neutralized *all* those formations which we have not incorporated, but this is not likely to be the case. The methods that we will follow to 'isolate' those formations that we have not been able to penetrate will be discussed in Chapter 4.

The degree of success required of our infiltration programme before we can proceed to the operational phase will depend on the military, political and geographical factors involved; the same degree of penetration may ensure success in one country while being inadequate in another. In our Portuguese example, because of the extensive deployment of the active troops in the remote African 'provinces', and the lack of training and mechanization of the troops stationed in Portugal, we could go ahead with minimal penetration (Table 8).

TABLE 8. *Infiltration of the Armed Forces in Portugal (notional)*

Total armed forces (Army, Navy and Air Force)	150,000
Incorporated as active participants:	3,000
Neutralized by the subversion of 'key' technicians:	12,000
Neutralized by unsuitable training and equipment:	45,000
Neutralized by their location: Angola	45,000
Mozambique	25,000
Portuguese Guinea	20,000
	150,000

This is an extreme example of a small and poor country which is trying to retain its African empire to the bitter end, and is therefore only leaving a very small force in its own metropolitan territory. The degree of incorporation achieved here is only about two per cent, and yet the *coup* would not find any *military* opposition in its way, unless it failed to impose its authority within the time-span required to bring into Lisbon the troops stationed in the African provinces. (The fact that the present regime is far from universally popular would reinforce the favourable 'military' factors.)

If, however, we take the case of a developed country with good transport links and with no overseas commitments for its troops, the same percentages of incorporation and active neutralization which in the Portuguese case would guarantee success would lead to certain failure, as illustrated in Table 9.

TABLE 9. *Infiltration of the Armed Forces in West Germany (notional)*

Total armed forces (Army, Navy and Air Force)	450,000
Incorporated as active participants:	9,000
Neutralized by the subversion of 'key' technicians:	40,000*
Neutralized by unsuitable equipment (mainly Air Force and Navy):	180,000
Balance of forces under the control of the Government:	221,000
	450,000

Since there is nothing that we can do to prevent the large forces capable of intervention from doing so, we would almost certainly fail – unless we *were* the higher leadership of the armed forces.

Most situations will be between the two extremes, with a small percentage of the armed forces incorporated, a larger percentage neutralized by our efforts, and a very small percentage to be 'isolated' by severing from the outside its communication and transport facilities. Apart from the military forces, the government will also be defended by police forces and their para-military extensions, and we now turn to the problem of their neutralization.

NEUTRALIZING THE POLICE

The flags and uniforms of the military forces of different countries are very different but their structure and organization tend to be very similar, since they reflect the universality of modern technology. The tactical implications of weapons and ancillary equipment impose a certain uniformity on military organization

*In a densely populated area, with extensive civilian telecommunication facilities and a highly developed transport system, even this figure could only be reached with very great efforts.

and this has enabled us to study their infiltration in terms which are generally applicable.

Police forces, however, are shaped by the social and political conditions of the society they serve and are therefore very diverse. Policemen can be armed very heavily or not at all; they can be concentrated in mobile and hard-hitting units, or dispersed in small groups; they can be controlled by the Ministry of Defence, and thus have a military training and outlook, or by the local community, and be extremely civilian-minded.

Though their structure is so diverse, police forces resemble each other in the purposes they serve: the prevention and the detection of crime* and the maintenance of public order. The criminal side of police work involves the country-wide network of police stations supported by special detective units in the larger centres. The maintenance of public order, however, is carried out by separate para-military forces or, where there are no such forces, by concentrating and deploying ordinary police-men taken from their other work. Police work also includes an intelligence element. Information is gathered informally by the entire police apparatus (and their informers), but there will usually be a special section of the police whose only function is in this area. The intelligence aspect of police work will be effectively neutralized by our general defensive effort, *vis-à-vis* the security services, which is discussed in the next section.

Para-military forces do not exist in Britain, where there are provisions for the army to act in support of the civil power, but they are extensively employed in many other countries. In France, for example, there are two police forces – the *Sûreté Nationale* and the *Préfecture de Police* – but there is also a para-military force which normally acts as the rural police, the *Gendarmerie*.†

The *Gendarmerie* is controlled by the Ministry of Defence and

---

*By crime is meant an infraction of the laws of the land, and this means different things in different countries – e.g. South African residential and Soviet publication laws.

† In the spring of 1968 the *Préfecture de Police* was administratively merged with the *Sûreté*.

its officers are integrated in the ranks of the armed forces, while the men receive a light infantry training as well as their police training. It numbers about 63,000 men, and is organized into departmental forces which are scattered in small groups all over the countryside and into 'mobile' groups which are concentrated in large units (Legions). We can ignore the departmental forces because they would probably be unable to intervene within the short time-span of a *coup*: but the mobile units, each of which consists of seven squadrons of trucked *gendarmes* and one armoured car squadron, represent a very formidable force that would have to be neutralized or isolated.

The mobile *Gendarmerie* live in military-type barracks and are equipped with sub-machine-guns and heavier infantry weapons; their armoured cars (13-ton wheeled vehicles with 40-mm armour) can only be stopped with standard anti-tank weaponry. Officially, the *Gendarmerie* – unlike the other two police forces – has no intelligence service; but during the Algerian war a security section was set up and, as bureaucratic organizations often do, has survived the demise of its original function.

The *Sûreté Nationale*, which carries out police work in population centres of more than 10,000 inhabitants (except for Paris and its suburbs), is largely composed of CID men and dispersed policemen, but it also has a para-military force. This is the *Compagnie Républicaine de Sécurité* (CRS). It numbers about 13,500 men, and they are trained and equipped in a manner like that of the mobile units of the *Gendarmerie* – minus the armoured cars. The CRS is staffed with personnel which has been carefully screened politically and it is headed by an assistant director of the Ministry of the Interior. The *Sûreté* has an intelligence service which largely concentrates on the more sophisticated forms of crime, and a counter-intelligence service which also carries out 'political' work and the surveillance of aliens. Both intelligence organizations operate all over France, including Paris,* unlike the rest of the *Sûreté*.

All police work in the *Départment de la Seine* (the Paris area)

*But, in Paris, the jurisdiction of the *Sûreté's intelligence* service is officially limited to the railway stations.

is the exclusive province of the *Préfecture de Police*, which has been made internationally famous by one of its fictional inspectors, Maigret. The *Préfecture* has influenced the organization of police forces in many countries in southern Europe and the Middle East, and we will study it in greater detail than the other French police forces.

Anatomy of a Police Force: The Paris Préfecture

Hopefully, the police of the capital city which is the locale of the *coup* will be less powerful than this force. It consists of about 24,000 men and is organized in several directorates, of which the following concern us directly:

(*a*) *The Police Municipale* is the largest directorate and controls the familiar uniformed *flics*, with their largely symbolic pistols and their much-used truncheons. They are dispersed in twenty district stations in the city and twenty-six suburban ones; their standards of training and discipline have been improved under the Vth Republic, but their capacity for individual brutality does not add up to effective intervention units. In the event of a major disturbance they are deployed in columns of civilian-type buses which could be stopped by suitable roadblocks; their training and mentality will probably make them 'neutrals' if we can prevent their concentrated deployment.

(*b*) *The Police Judiciaire* is the Paris CID and one of the pioneers of scientific detection. Apart from the incidental intelligence aspect of their work, we can ignore this directorate.

(*c*) *The Intelligence service,* like its counterpart in the *Sûreté,* is mainly concerned with sophisticated crime: drugs, vice and high-class gambling. But it also has a political section which carries out surveillance work. As in the case of other security agencies, we will cover the appropriate defensive tactics in the next section.

(*d*) *Aliens' directorate* is a small group, mainly concerned with the bureaucratic routines of issuing and checking residence permits. It exercises general surveillance over transient foreigners (the *fiches* you fill in at the hotel are collected by this directorate), and over foreign communities. Its work will only affect us if we have some connexion with foreign elements, and particularly with those foreign communities which have a history of political activity in its more violent forms.

(e) *Safety of the President.* This directorate is concerned with the physical protection of the President, but it also carries out a preventive intelligence function. Following the repeated assassination attempts organized by the OAS and its affiliated organizations, this section of the *Préfecture* was reinforced with carefully screened personnel taken from the entire security apparatus. Their security system at the Élysée Palace would be a serious obstacle to its seizure during a *coup*.

(f) *Garde Républicaine.* Though controlled by the *Préfecture*, this is part of the *Gendarmerie* and is equipped with light infantry weapons and a variety of transport equipment. It provides the horsed, helmeted and plumed Presidential guard on ceremonial occasions, but its two regiments are hard-hitting mobile forces whose neutralization would be an essential requirement in the event of a *coup*.

The existence of separate police organizations is one of the problems of neutralizing this part of the state security apparatus. In Britain, the division is largely territorial and its purpose is to give the local interest a measure of control over the police force, but there are also specialized forces which reflect functional divisions. Apart from the county-based police (now being amalgamated into larger groups) there are the following independent police forces:

> Admiralty constabulary
> Air Ministry constabulary
> Atomic Energy Authority constabulary
> Five independent harbour police forces
> British Transport Commission police
> Civil aviation constabulary
> War Department constabulary

All these police forces are strictly confined in their operations to the installations they protect, but similar organizations in other countries, where bureaucratic propensities are subject to weaker controls, have shown a remarkable ability to grow and diversify.

Though the French police system is particularly extensive, its basic features are shared by police forces in most of Africa, Asia and the Middle East. The para-military element is usually present in the form of a 'field force' attached to the regular police, or else in the form of armoured car units. The riot-control element is reproduced in the special squads of Middle Eastern police forces which, like Beirut's Squad 16, can be very effective in spite of their small size. Where, as in most parts of Asia, a serious insurgency situation has been experienced, this common pattern has been distorted by the proliferation of *ad hoc* police forces which carry out combined internal security and administrative functions. South Vietnam is the extreme example of this trend, with no fewer than five different formations.*

If the British police system can be said to be divided into largely territorial units, and the French one into largely functional ones, in the United States the division is largely constitutional. Except for the specialized work of the police agencies attached to various departments of the federal government, only the FBI has a nation-wide jurisdiction and then only for certain crimes legally defined as 'federal'. Most ordinary police work is carried out by purely independent local forces maintained at the municipal, county or state level. The fragmentation† of the system means that the police as such would have a very limited intervention potential, in spite of its extensive stock of weaponry and communication equipment. There is, of course, the National Guard, but this has not so far been organized in a manner that would give it a real intervention capability, as was shown by the

*Regional Forces (about 100,000 men), Popular Forces (about 30,000 men), Civilian Irregular Defence Groups (about 20,000 men), the regular police, and the supposedly *élite* Police Field Force.

†Of course the fragmentation of the police in the United States has largely resulted from the *deliberate intention* of denying the federal government a possible instrument of tyranny. Nowadays, however, the main effect of the system is to impede efficient police work, viz. the case of the 'Boston Strangler'.

events of the summer of 1967 when the Guard failed to perform efficiently, even against untrained civilians.

The strategy of the *coup*, with respect to the police system of our target country will, therefore, have to be as diversified as its component parts:

The Para-Military Element

Para-military forces are usually able to perform a military as well as a police function. This versatility has resulted in their rapid growth, partly because they may be a genuinely economical way of improving the security system in general, and partly because funds are often easier to secure for them than for the regular police. An opposition party, or public opinion, which may resist an increase in the police budget can often be persuaded to allocate funds for the Ministry of Defence, and para-military forces are usually under its administrative control. In the newly-independent countries the para-military element of the police can be a very serious obstacle to the *coup* because, while the army is often a recent post-colonial development, the police – and its para-military units – are usually old-established organizations. This means that the police can be *larger* than the army, and also sometimes superior in the quality of training and equipment. If this is the case, it will not be possible to control the para-military units by using that part of the army which we have 'incorporated' against them.

Fortunately, the governments of newly-independent countries are making every effort to increase the size of their armed forces and thus this unfavourable (for us) balance of strength between the army and the para-military police is usually reversed a few years after independence. This is perhaps one of the explanations for the sudden spate of *coups* in Africa in the course of 1966–7, which came after a phase of very rapid expansion in the armed forces. It is interesting to note that, while the 'ruthless oppression' of the colonial powers was often carried out by means of a village constabulary with few military pretensions, the new era of freedom has often required the creation of heavily armed para-military police forces.* In Ghana, for example, the

★But see Appendix A.

police system was extended after independence in 1957 and armoured car units were added to the already existing mobile police; the communication system of the police was made independent of civilian services, and the 'Escort police', which used to be a fezzed and barefooted force of amiable illiterates, has been turned into an effective riot-breaking unit.

If the para-military police is large, as compared to those units of the armed forces which we can incorporate, it will be necessary to repeat the whole analysis and infiltration procedure on it. We may, indeed, be able to concentrate on the para-military police and content ourselves with neutralizing the army by technical means. Normally, however, the balance of forces between the means of coercion of the state will not require this and we will be able to *isolate* the police for the duration of the *coup* by using the army.

The first step in our neutralization of these forces is to establish the size, deployment and organization of the para-military police. This is usually easier than in the case of the army because, unlike the latter, para-military forces are usually stationed in permanent barracks. Next we will try to find out their degree of attachment to the present regime. But this will not involve the sort of study in depth we made of the army, and it will only be a matter of finding out about their *corporate*, rather than individual outlook. The mentality of the para-military police may be 'bureaucratic', i.e. concerned with jobs and careers – as in the case of the Italian *Pubblica Sicurezza* and its *Celere* para-military units; if this is the case, a minimal degree of intervention can be expected. On the other hand, their mentality may be parallel to that of the army, i.e. concerned with loyalty and honour* (as well as jobs and careers) or reflect a political association, as in the case of the KBG or Duvalier's Ton Ton Macoutes.

If the equipment, deployment and mentality of the para-military police is such as to make them an effective intervention force we will have to control them in the same manner as the 'hard core' loyalist forces of the army. (The ways and means of this forcible isolation will be discussed in Chapter 5.) Usually,

---

*The corporate mentality will of course be somewhat more complex than is suggested here by way of illustration.

however, we will find that the para-military police force is essentially bureaucratic and, therefore, in spite of its impressive military bearing and equipment, it will not intervene against the armed support of a *coup*. I have been unable to find a *single case* in the last twenty years of a para-military police which has actually defended its political masters during a *coup* – though there are several cases of their intervention *on behalf* of a *coup*.

The Rural Police and Gendarmerie

In most underdeveloped countries, this element of the police force is numerically the strongest; this is only to be expected since most of the population of such countries lives in villages and works in agriculture. In spite of its large size, this part of the police will almost never have an intervention potential against a *coup*. They are often retired NCOs, fully integrated in the rural society they live in and, even where there are provisions for their mobilization and concentrated use, they are unlikely to be assembled, equipped and prepared in time to intervene against us. Whether the rural policeman is a *garde champêtre* with an ancient pistol inscribed *La Loi*, or a Middle Eastern *Zaptie* who plays the village boss, he will hardly want to rush to a remote capital city to protect an equally remote government.

The Urban and National Police

Though this part of the police system will be considerably less dispersed than the village-based rural police, its main components will be just as ineffective against a *coup*. The personnel of the urban police will fall into three broad categories: (*a*) crime detection and investigation; (*b*) normal surveillance, and (*c*) traffic duties. The CID element will be small, very bureaucratic-minded and, apart from its incidental intelligence aspect,* it can be ignored by us. The uniformed police which carries out all the usual surveillance duties will be more numerous, but though they may be useful as a riot-breaking force when suitably

* See next section, p. 99.

concentrated they are unlikely to act against *armed* opponents in a major political crisis. The municipal police, largely concerned with traffic duties, will usually be staffed by middle-aged men of retiring disposition, with small and rusty pistols. There are, however, exceptions such as the Spanish *Policía Armada y del Tráfico* whose personnel are politically screened and which is equipped with adequate transport and telecommunications and thus able (and probably willing) to intervene in a major political disturbance. A detailed analysis of our target country's police system will probably reveal a problem of composition: after dividing the police force into 'hard' and 'soft' forces we may find sizeable 'hard' sub-divisions within the 'soft' elements.

Our brief survey has shown that only a small part of the police force is likely to be able to intervene against us, and of this a yet smaller part is likely to do so with any enthusiasm. The natural inclination of the police will be to 'ride' the crisis out and, as individuals, to avoid endangering their positions *vis-à-vis* their possible future employers. The *coup* may well be planned as a military operation, but it will not – unless partially or totally unsuccessful – involve any actual *fighting*. Thus, the fact that the police is not heavily armed does not fundamentally explain their low intervention capability, as compared to the army. The real difference between the two is in their degree of integration in the civil society. While the army can develop a corporate ideology and mentality which is divergent – or even opposed – to the civilian one, the police is usually too intimately involved in civilian life to do so.

This can be either an advantage or an obstacle from our point of view. On the one hand the eccentricity of the army will mean that a regime can retain its appeal in the closed world of the military barracks after losing it in society at large. This might interfere with our recruiting, but it could work the other way, i.e. we may find that the army is fundamentally opposed to a government which much civilian opinion accepts. Recruiting our forces among the police will almost always be more difficult than in the army. Firstly, the lower level of (automatic) discipline will mean that recruiting an officer may not bring over 'his' men as well. Further, the fact that policemen live among the public will mean that the internal dynamics which can be generated in the closed world of a military unit would be dissipated in this more open environment and the 'snow-ball' effect which would bring entire units over to us after a limited degree of infiltration will not operate. All these factors point the same way: the low degree of intervention capability – for, as well as against us – and the difficulty of incorporation, both indicate that while the army should be penetrated the police forces can be dealt with – defensively – after the *coup*.

NEUTRALIZING THE SECURITY AGENCIES

The security agencies of our target country will be numerically the smallest of the professional defences of the state, but often also the most dangerous. Unlike the armed forces and the police, the security agencies will be actively trying to identify and defeat threats posed by groups such as ours; unlike the armed forces and police, their organizations, deployment and personnel cannot usually be studied from the outside, and even their existence may not be known to us. Almost every state has some sort of 'secret service'. Many have several such organizations which operate both within and outside the national territory, and which we have so far described with the blanket term of 'security agencies'. Our first task is to try to identify them more precisely.

It is well known that the bureaucratic animal in its natural state has certain characteristic patterns of behaviour: it grows in size and extends its sphere of action until checked by some outside force. This role is usually played by the financial bureaucracy, which fulfils its instincts by opposing the growth of all other bureaucratic organizations. Equally important as a limiting factor, is the concerted pressure of individual bureaucracies, each of which is fighting to preserve and extend its territory. The cumulative effect of these pressures is to limit to some extent the growth of the bureaucracy as a whole, and perhaps without them *all* the inhabitants of developed countries would by now be employed by the state bureaucracy.

These pressures operate weakly or not at all in the case of the security services: their budgets are allocated by many different departments and are usually secret so that they cannot easily be known, let alone reduced; other bureaucratic organizations cannot prevent them from poaching in their territories because their activities cannot often be identified and thus declared to be off-limits. Finally, the prestige which undercover men of all kinds often enjoy allows them to break rules which other bureaucrats must obey, and to operate in all areas of social activity. The result of this freedom is predictable: in many countries security agencies have grown in a more dynamic and more disorderly fashion than the rest of the bureaucracy and tend to have overlapping spheres of activity.

Before a zoologist studies his animals he classifies them and tries to relate them to the nearest known species. We will follow this procedure both in functional terms (which are generally applicable to all countries) and in organizational terms (which are particular to each one).

The Pure Intelligence Function

This classification covers the collection and analysis of published and unpublished information of all kinds and, because of the high degree of specialized knowledge which is often required, many different bodies can enter this field, which is the most crowded of the whole sector. *Tactical* military intelligence (What is the opposition doing?) may be collected by separate agencies working for the three branches of the armed forces; in traditionally seafaring nations, naval intelligence is often the largest and most developed service. *Strategic* information (What is the opposition planning?) may be the province of separate and competing agencies run by the General Staff, the Ministry of Defence and the ministry in charge of foreign affairs. *Scientific* information may be collected by the administrative entity in charge of 'science' and also by specialized bodies in charge of particular sectors, such as atomic energy, aeronautics and telecommunications. *Economic* intelligence is one of the worst areas of duplication, with demographic, energy and agriculture authorities operating alongside the entity in charge of economic affairs in general. *Political* intelligence may be handled by the foreign affairs ministry openly, through the diplomatic service and also covertly by a separate agency.

The Counter-Intelligence Function

This covers the prevention of the activities listed above and may be carried out by both generalized and specialized bodies. The military may run their own agency, and the police of each branch of the armed forces may do the same. The Ministry of the Interior will almost always have a 'spy-catching' service (like the Security Service of the Home Office) and particular bodies will have a service to protect their installations (but these rarely go beyond the ordinary police stage). From our point of view, this sector will be the most important. We may – if we fail to preserve our security position – come into contact with (a) the police agency, such as Special Branch in Britain or the FBI in the USA, (b) the separate ministerial body, or (c) the military agencies. Much of our planning and infiltration work will be indistinguishable from that which could be carried out by a foreign intelligence service and it will therefore enter into the territory of the counter-intelligence agencies.

The Counter-Espionage Function

This is the most subtle and sophisticated of all the functions. It covers the deliberate contact with opposition intelligence services, in order to feed them with 'disinformation' or to disrupt their organization. It is unlikely that more than one agency carries out this work because it requires an extremely precise control over operations. The agency may be a subsection of any of those mentioned above, but in order to function efficiently it must be able to exercise some form of control over all competing agencies – especially over counter-intelligence, which relates to counter-espionage as a butcher does to a surgeon.

Internal (political) Security

This is another sensitive area from our point of view. Its specific function is the prevention of exactly what we aim to do: the overthrow of the government. In many countries there is a 'political' police, with both uniformed and covert agents, and it may be controlled by the bureaucracy of the Ministry of the Interior or by the inner political leadership, either directly or, in one-party states, through the party. Elsewhere, in more or less democratic regimes the police has a political department, as in France, Italy and West Germany, and its primary function is the surveillance of extremist groups. In military dictatorships, the territory of military intelligence often extends to this area; in some countries the agency in charge of the physical protection of the higher leadership may run an information service as well as providing the bodyguards.

Internal Intelligence

This function is carried out by the information services which are attached to the police and para-military forces of the state. Thus, in Italy, apart from the police (*Pubblica Sicurezza*) which has a 'political' squad, the para-military *Carabinieri* has an information service (SIFAR) which, though primarily concerned with military counter-intelligence, also operates in the internal political field.

Our behaviour in the midst of this bureaucratic jungle will be purely defensive, unless we have a 'direct line' to one or other of the security agencies. If that is the case, the security agency concerned would provide an ideal 'cover' for all our activities. Failing such a fortunate coincidence, we will not try to create a 'direct line' by infiltrating any security service, because if we do so there will be the very great danger that they will use any contact in order to infiltrate *us*. This is a standard procedure for the security services to follow, and the elementary defensive techniques used when infiltrating the armed forces (cut-outs, one-way communication etc.) will probably fail to work in their case.

In order to run a secure operation we will follow rules which derive from the basic assumption that *all* information about our activities is a source of danger as soon as it exists outside the minds of our inner group. From this all the standard procedures emerge: (*a*) no information to be communicated except verbally; (*b*) no information to be communicated except on a 'need-to-know' basis; (c) all communication links from inner to affiliated members to be on a one-way basis; (d) no activity to be carried out by an inner member if an outer member can do the job.

These rules are simple and well known; the problem is to keep to them under the pressure of work and the emotions which it generates. The most sensitive of our activities will be the approach and persuasion of new affiliates to the *coup*, and the nature of the security agencies can add an extra measure of danger: in many countries some of the security services are hidden within totally unexciting administrative bodies. Where, as in the case of the US Treasury's Secret Service, this reflects an administrative convenience, the fact is well known; elsewhere, however, the department-within-a-department system is deliberate. We may therefore unwittingly try to infiltrate a 'safe' department and discover that we are dealing with a security agency. All we can do is to list some of the places where it is 'natural' for security services to 'grow': census and cartography services; central bank anti-counterfeiting agencies; post office departments; press bureaux; customs and immigration departments and the taxation authorities.

It must not be thought that our entire operation will automatically collapse if it is penetrated by a security agency.* If we have followed the security procedures the chances are that only a small part of our total effort will be identified, and therefore its ultimate purpose may not be discovered. Even if it is discovered that a *coup* is being planned, the security agency may wait before taking any action, in order to capture *all* the planners – and this could be too late. As soon as our teams are on the road, actually executing the *coup*, it will be too late for the security services to oppose us on the 'information' side, while

---

*The Okhrana, the Tzarist secret police, was extremely efficient and it had infiltrated the Bolshevik and other revolutionary parties without, however, impairing their activities. Roman Malinovsky, who was the leader of the Bolshevik organization inside Russia until 1914, was working for the Okhrana, and *they* edited *Pravda*, whose chief editor was also one of their agents. This, incidentally, later lent some slight plausibility to the accusations made at the Moscow trials, that old Bolshevik leaders had been lifelong stooges of foreign secret services (usually the British).

their fighting power will usually be unimportant as compared to the army units we have incorporated. Finally, political security agencies are necessarily sensitive to political trends, and they may decide to join the group planning a *coup* if they know that it is well organized and ready to seize power.

4. The Planning of the *Coup d'État*

'... Even barricades, apparently a mechanical element of the uprising, are of significance in reality above all as a moral force ...' *Lev Davidovich Bronstein (Trotsky)*

In the early morning of 23 April 1961, elements of the 1st Foreign Legion Parachute Regiment seized the key points of the city of Algiers in the name of Generals Challe, Zeller, Jouhaud and Salan. The four generals, because of their personal prestige and their position in the French hierarchy, quickly asserted their control over the local military command and started to extend their authority over all the armed forces in Algeria. At this time de Gaulle's government was in the process of opening negotiations with the Algerian nationalists and the generals were determined to replace him with a leader who would carry the war to a victorious conclusion. The French armed forces in Algeria were much more powerful than those stationed in France and Germany and the four generals were hopeful that, once their allegiance was assured, they would find it easy to take effective control of the French government. After all, de Gaulle himself had come to power after a similar episode in May 1958, and there seemed to be no major obstacle to a successful second edition of the famous *treize mai*.

When the four generals made their declaration over Algiers Radio, the 1st, 14th and 18th Colonial Parachute regiments rallied to the *coup*. A few infantry units, some of the Marines and much of the Air Force remained loyal to de Gaulle (as in May 1958 they had remained loyal to the IVth Republic), but most of the armed forces in Algeria were *attentiste*. Wait-and-see is the attitude that usually favours a *coup* and when General

Henri de Pouilly withdrew his headquarters from Oran to Tlemcen, to avoid having to choose between fighting or joining the *coup*, he was objectively favouring the *coup*.

The four generals seemed to be on the verge of victory. The determined *pieds noirs* population of Algeria was 100 per cent behind them. The powerful parachute units gave them a hard-hitting force of intervention and the bulk of the armed forces were either for them or neutral. Even the forces loyal to de Gaulle's government did nothing actively to oppose the *coup*.

While the leaders of the *coup* started to gather support, the French Defence Minister was on a visit to Morocco; Maurice Papon, the head of the Paris police, was on vacation; Debré, the Prime Minister and chief 'fire-fighter' of the regime, was ill; de Gaulle himself was entertaining the visiting President of Senegal, Senghor. Other ministers were on visits to Algiers itself, and were promptly captured and held in confinement, together with other representatives of the President. Everything pointed to an early victory of the *coup*, and yet a few days later General Challe was being flown to Paris for eventual trial and imprisonment, Salan and the others were fleeing to the interior on their way to exile or capture, and the 1st Foreign Legion Parachute Regiment drove back to their barracks singing Edith Piaf's '*Je ne regrette rien*', though their officers were under arrest and their unit was to be disbanded.

Why did the *coup* fail? Perhaps the main reason was that the four generals had utterly neglected the 'political forces' and had allowed the immediate power of the armed forces to obscure the somewhat less immediate, but ultimately decisive, role that they could play. In the Gaullist *coup* of May 1958, the action of the military and the population of Algiers had been supported by the Gaullist infiltration of the civil service, and by the steady corrosion of the will of other political groups to oppose the dissolution of the IVth Republic. This time the generals had simply ignored the civilians.

De Gaulle went on television and called for popular support: '*Françaises, Français, aidez-moi.*' Debré, who followed him on the screen, was more specific: 'Go . . . to the airports . . . convince the soldiers who are misled . . .' He also started to arm a militia drawn from the Gaullist party. More important, the trade-union organizations, the Communists (CGT), the Christian Democrats (CFTC), and the *Force Ouvrière,* all rallied round the government while most political parties did the same; the left-wing Catholic movement started to organize sit-down strikes among the national servicemen in Algeria; and, in general, most organized forces of French society intervened and refused to accept the authority of the *coup.*

The effect of this refusal was decisive; the larger part of the 'wait-and-see' element in the armed forces stopped waiting and declared its support for de Gaulle, and this was the end of the *coup.*

We will only be able to avoid a repetition of the crucial error made by the generals if we can neutralize the political forces as effectively as the military ones.

Immediate political power is always concentrated in the country's government, but in every country and under all political systems there will be groups outside the government – and even outside formal politics – which also have political power. Their source of strength can be their ability to influence, particular groups of voters (as in democratic societies) or their control over certain organizations which are important in the country's political life. Whether these groups, which we have called 'the political forces', are pressure groups, political parties or other associations does not greatly matter. What is of importance is their ability to participate in the formation of governments, and, later, to influence their decisions. The nature of the forces which are important in the political life of a particular country will reflect the structure of its society and economy, and it will also depend on the particular context of decision-making.

If, for example, we were asked to list the most important forces in British political life, we could produce the following (rather conventional) list:

the two major political parties
the Trades Union Congress and certain major unions
the Confederation of British Industry
the senior civil-service–academic complex

the City and its corporations
the press

But if we were asked to isolate the groups which would matter in foreign policy decision about, say, the Middle East, we would come up with a quite different list:

the two major British and part-British oil companies
the Foreign Office–academic 'Arabist' group
the central organizations of British Jews

TABLE 10. *The groups which would influence the formation of American policy on Middle Eastern questions. Formal and unofficial participants.*

Official:

the President and the White House staff
the Department of State
the Pentagon
the CIA (as supplier of information)
the key Congressional Committees

Unofficial:

(a) Oil companies with interests in the Middle East. (These seek to protect and extend their interests and therefore advocate sympathetic understanding for Arab aspirations and policies.)

(b) Oil companies with exclusively domestic interests. (These favour a continuation of the existing policy of excluding foreign oil from the US market, and are therefore inimical to any general US – Arab *rapprochement*.)

(c) Other energy industries. (Which also oppose any relaxation of present US import controls on – cheap – foreign oil.)

(d) Politicians with significant Jewish populations in their constituencies. (These naturally follow a visible pro-Israel line on Congressional voting and make appropriate speeches.)

(e) Pro-Zionist organizations of American Jewry.

(f) American Council for Judaism. (This body is anti-Zionist and opposes the pro-Israel elements in this field.)

(g) Academic bodies with a special interest in Arab or Middle Eastern studies. (These usually identify with Arab views and seek a sympathetic hearing of Arab claims.)

In a sophisticated society, with its complex industrial and social structure, there are hundreds of organizations which, whatever their primary purpose, also act as pressure groups and attempt to influence political decisions in a manner that serves their members' interests. These organizations will reflect in their divergent attitudes the diversity of a complex society. In economically backward countries, however, the structure of society is simpler and any conflict of interests, though just as strong, is played out in a much smaller arena and with fewer participants. In Africa south of the Sahara religious groups are generally fragmented and apolitical, and where the local business community is still relatively small and weak, the major political forces are limited to a few groupings:

Tribal and other ethnic groups
Trade unions
Students' and graduates' associations
Civil-service officials and officers of the armed forces
The activists of the ruling political party

In much of West Africa one would have to add the local market traders' association, and in immediate sub-Saharan areas the traditional Muslim leadership structures. In Asia, religious groups and their leaders would have to be added to the list, and in some countries (such as Taiwan, Thailand, South Korea and Hong Kong) the local business class will be of importance. Missing from all the lists are the foreign business interests which may play an important or even dominant role, but which represent a special problem already dealt with in Chapter 2. But whatever groups dominate the political scene of our target country in normal times, the special circumstances of the *coup* will mean that only a few elements among them will be important to us.

Political forces can intervene against the *coup* in two ways:

(*a*) they can rally and deploy the masses, or some part of them, against the new government;

(*b*) they can manipulate technical facilities under their control in order to oppose the consolidation of our power.

The action of individual political, religious, ethnic or intellectual leaders, who could use the framework of their party or community against us, is an example of the first kind of intervention; a strike of the staff of the radio-television service is an example of the second. A general strike would, in effect, combine both kinds of intervention.

Neutralizing the Political Forces I: general

Politics, like economics, has its infrastructure. Just as industry and commerce require a background of facilities such as roads, ports and energy sources, direct political action requires certain technical facilities. The mobilization of French public opinion which took place during the attempted *coup* in Algiers – and which was the principal cause of its failure – could not have taken place without the use of a whole range of technical facilities. The government appealed to public opinion by means of the mass media, chiefly the radio and television services; the trade unions and other organized bodies coordinated the agitation of their members by means of their network of branches, connected to the central headquarters by means of the public telecommunications facilities; finally the mass demonstrations could not have taken place without the use of public and private transport.

Our *general* neutralization of the 'political' forces will be conducted in terms of this infrastructure. We will seize and hold such facilities as we require for our own purposes, while temporarily putting out of action the others. If the means of communication and the transport system are under our control, or at any rate do not function, the potential threat posed by the 'political forces' will be largely neutralized: the leaders of the pre-*coup* government will be arrested since they are part of the infrastructure and they would probably be the major sources of inspiration of any opposition to the *coup*.*

We will neutralize some political forces in *particular* by identifying and isolating their leadership, and by disrupting

---

*In seizing the leaders of the government we will also contribute towards the isolation of those segments of the army and police which we have been unable to infiltrate, though more direct measures will be required as well.

their organizations; this will only be necessary for those forces which are sufficiently resilient and sufficiently militant to intervene against us even though the infrastructure has been neutralized.

Both forms of neutralization will involve the selection of certain objectives which will be seized or put out of action, by teams* formed out of those forces of the state which we have fully subverted or, in our terminology, incorporated.

Unless our target country is particularly small and its physical and political structures particularly simple, its system of government will be complex, its physical facilities will be extensive, and its political forces will be many in number while their intervention capabilities will be difficult to forecast.

We will, therefore, start by analysing the governmental leadership in order to determine which personalities will have to be isolated for the duration of the active phase of the *coup* and which can be safely ignored. Next, we will study the physical facilities and select those which are likely to be relevant during the *coup*, in order to plan their seizure or neutralization. Finally, we will investigate the likely nature of those political forces which could still retain a degree of intervention capability after our 'general' measures, in order to prepare for their individual neutralization.

PERSONALITIES IN THE GOVERNMENT

However bloodless our *coup*, however progressive and liberal our aims, we will still have to arrest certain individuals during and immediately after, its execution. Of these the most important group will be formed by the leading figures of the pre-*coup* regime or, in other words, the leaders of the government and their close associates, whether they are formally politicians or not. The members of a Cabinet will form a fairly large group, from ten to fifty people; adding their associates and intimate advisers – who could organize opposition against us – we could easily reach a figure four or five times this number. Apart from being uncomfortably large, this will also be an especially

---

*The nature and composition of the active teams of the *coup* are discussed in Appendix B.

determined and dangerous group. The personal repute, presence and authority of its members could be such as to enable them to rally against us the disorganized forces of the state, or the unorganized masses: it could also enable them to impose their will on the team sent to capture them, and turn their would-be captors into their allies. General Challe, for example, was regarded as the *patron* by the NCOs of the French Army in Algeria, and even after the total failure of his attempted *coup*, the Paris government could not entrust him to a military escort on his way to France and arrest, and had to use the CRS,* who had never experienced his personal authority. After all, if a young soldier acting outside his familiar roles is facing a political personality whose whole behaviour is calculated to make people obey him, it is difficult to be absolutely certain that he will carry out his orders, and not the counter-orders he may be given.

The large number of the separate targets, and the possible 'radiation' effects, indicate that the teams sent to arrest them should be both large and particularly well chosen. Since our resources will be limited, we will have to concentrate our efforts on the most important figures within the group while leaving the others to be picked up later when our means will have been expanded by the allegiance of the 'wait-and-see' element. We cannot arrest all those who may constitute an eventual danger, but we must make sure that we do arrest the really dangerous figures, that is, the key figures within the leadership, who may or may not be the first in the formal order of precedence.

The formal structure of governments falls into two broad categories (illustrated in Table 10): the 'presidential' type, where the head of state is also the main decision-maker (as in the USA, France and most of the Afro-Asian states), and the 'prime-ministerial' type, where the head of state has largely symbolic or ceremonial duties and real decision-making is carried out at a theoretically lower level (as in Britain, India and most of Europe, as well as the USSR).

A third alternative form – which is not a structure at all, but rather a denial of one – is the 'strong man' form of government.

*Compagnies Républicaines de Sécurité, part of the police and outside the military community.

TABLE II. *Alternative Forms of Government*

Presidential

Real decision-making level:
- King (e.g. seventeenth-century England)
- President (e.g. twentieth-century America)
- Emperor (e.g. twentieth-century Ethiopia)
- Ruler (e.g. twentieth-century Kuwait)

Prime (or Chief) Minister
Ministerial level
Junior ministers and civil service

Prime-ministerial

Ceremonial head of State:
- King (e.g. Belgium)
- President (e.g. Italy)

Real decision-making level:
- Prime Minister (e.g. United Kingdom)
- President of Council of Ministers (e.g. Italy)

Cabinet level ministers
Junior ministers
Higher civil servants

The 'strong man' may not be a top minister, and may hold no official position at all, but actually rules by using the formal body of politicians as a screen. This type of regime is evolved when the fabric of the state has been weakened to such an extent that only the actual leader of some part of the armed forces or police can control the situation and remain in power. If the person is himself even minimally acceptable as a political leader, he can take over the formal posts as well and make himself the visible head of the government. Abd-el-Nasir in Egypt, and Reza Shah (the father of the present Shah of Persia) both accomplished this after a short period of transition, but there can sometimes be racial or religious reasons that bar the 'strong man' from an official position. The man who controls the bayonets may be totally unacceptable as a public figure, but he can still rule indirectly by manipulating the official leaders which he keeps under control by the ultimate sanction of force.

When in early 1966 the Syrian government of the moderate wing of the Ba'ath party, headed by Michel Aflak, Salah Bitar and the army leader Hafiz, was overthrown by an extreme left faction of the party, the new leadership found out that though it controlled the army and the country it could not rule openly. The army officers who led this latest *coup* were too young, too unknown and, above all, they were Alawites. Salah Jadid, their leader, is a dark, brooding figure who inspired fear and hatred among that small part of the public that knew of him. And of all the communities of Syria, the Alawites are amongst the least prestigious. In colonial times the French had recruited most of their forces of repression, the *Troupes spéciales du Levant*, from the minority communities, chiefly the Alawites, and they had given the Alawite area in northern Syria a form of autonomy in order – so the Nationalists claimed – to break up Syrian national unity. After independence the Sunni majority community regarded the Alawites as renegades, and public opinion would only have accepted an Alawite head of state with difficulty.

Salah Jadid overcame this problem by appointing a full set of Cabinet Ministers, carefully chosen so as to balance the various communities, while retaining the real decision-making power within a separate body, 'the National Revolutionary Council', headed by himself. Thus, though Syria has a President (Nurredin Atassi), a Prime Minister (Youssof Zwayeen), and a Foreign Minister (Ibrahim Makhous), all major political decisions are made by Jadid; the ministers go on state visits, make the public speeches and appear in all ceremonial occasions, but power is not in their hands.

The government of the 'socialist' countries is formally party government, but it tends to break down into one of the two other types. In its original form, real political power is concentrated in the hands of the central committee, or some other higher party council, as illustrated in Figure 1.

Once the purely ceremonial figures have been excluded, the number of people still to be dealt with will be reduced, and by applying our time-span criterion, we can reduce their numbers still further. The Minister of Economic Planning may be a crucial figure in the government, his position as a technocrat may be unassailable, but he may be unable to rally public opinion against us, or to assert his authority over the armed forces. The dramatic nature of the *coup* will reduce political life

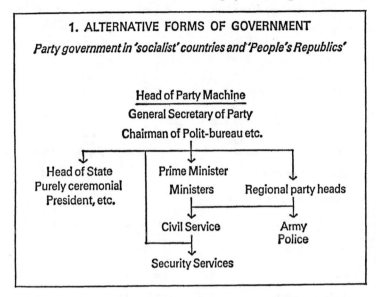

1. ALTERNATIVE FORMS OF GOVERNMENT

Party government in 'socialist' countries and 'People's Republics'

Head of Party Machine
General Secretary of Party
Chairman of Polit-bureau etc.

Head of State
Purely ceremonial
President, etc.

Prime Minister
Ministers

Regional party heads

Civil Service

Army
Police

Security Services

to its ultimate rationale, sheer force, and we will concentrate on those figures in the government who could deploy it. The obvious personalities will therefore be:

(*a*) the Minister of the Interior and his associates (who control the police force);

(*b*) the Minister of Defence and his associates (who control the armed forces);

(*c*) the party leaders (if there is a party militia);

(*d*) the Prime Minister or other central figure (who coordinates all these).

We must remember that for various reasons figures in the government may not always be what they appear to be. We may discover that the apparently innocuous Minister of Education controls an important students' militia, or the Minister of Labour a powerful workers' militia. More important, the effective power may be held by an inner association of a particular group of ministers who between them control the means of coercion of the state. Thus, the government of Czechoslovakia between the elections of May 1946 and the final Communist

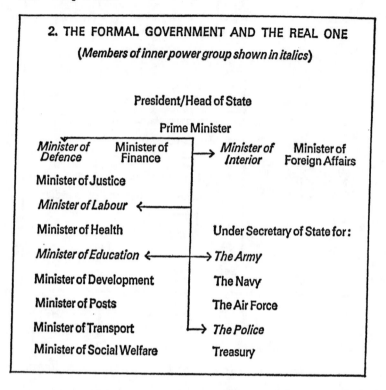

2. THE FORMAL GOVERNMENT AND THE REAL ONE

(Members of inner power group shown in italics)

President/Head of State

Prime Minister

| *Minister of Defence* | Minister of Finance | *Minister of Interior* | Minister of Foreign Affairs |

Minister of Justice

Minister of Labour

Minister of Health

Minister of Education

Minister of Development

Minister of Posts

Minister of Transport

Minister of Social Welfare

Under Secretary of State for:

The Army

The Navy

The Air Force

The Police

Treasury

take-over in February 1948 was a coalition of all 'democratic' parties, but the Communist ministers within it effectively monopolized the real sources of power by means of the control of the means of coercion. The existence of a group of associates, whose alliance transcends the formal order of government, is illustrated in Figure 2.

In this particular case, out of the eighteen or so members of the government, the Prime Minister, the Ministers of Defence, Labour, Education and the Under Secretaries of State for the Army and Police, form a special inner council which actually holds the reins of power.

The process of selection so far discussed should result in the classification of the personalities of the pre-*coup* regime into three categories:

The Ceremonial Figures

These will not be arrested. If the head of state is generally popular he should be used as a symbol of continuity who will help us to establish our legitimacy, provided he can be safely manipulated and made to play this role. The other, lesser ceremonial figures can simply be ignored.

The 'inner council' and the Controllers of the Means of Coercion

This small group must be sequestrated and held in isolation until our authority is safely established. Apart from the service ministers, etc., any government leader who is personally particularly popular should be included in this category.

The Other Ministers and Top Civil Servants

This larger group should be subdivided into priority groups and put into the category above, as and when our resources expand, or become available when other more urgent tasks have been carried out.

PERSONALITIES OUTSIDE GOVERNMENT

The political weight of an individual in any large-scale political community will usually only be important within the framework of an organization which he heads or manipulates. It is sometimes possible for an individual to achieve political importance by becoming identified with an ideology or an attitude in which some significant part of the public believes. Kossuth, the leader of the Hungarian nationalist movement in the 1848–9 Revolution, was a poet by profession, and had no party machine behind him, but he did have considerable power because the masses (in the cities at any rate) identified his person with Hungarian nationalism. Gandhi, who operated largely outside the Congress party machine, also achieved personal power because to many Indians he was the embodiment of nationalism. The remoteness of the examples indicates that such figures are very rare, and if we do have them in our target area they should be treated as ceremonial figures.

PHYSICAL FACILITIES

Mass Media

Control over the flow of information emanating from the political centre will be our most important weapon in establishing our authority after the *coup*. The seizure of the main means of mass communication will thus be a task of crucial importance. One, though only one, of the causes of the failure of the Greek King's counter-*coup* in late 1967 was this inability to communicate with the masses, literally and otherwise. When Radio Larissa broadcast the King's messages it only reached a fraction of the population: the transmitter was weak and the wave-length unusual; instead of the booming voice of authority the declaration took the form of a weak appeal for help. We must not make a similar mistake.

Because of the short time-span of the *coup*, and because of the likely social background of our target country, the press need not be a primary target; we will establish our authority over it after the *coup*, as with other aspects of the nation's life. Inevitably the press can only play a marginal role in countries where illiteracy is widespread; and, in any case, it is the radio-television service which is mainly associated with the voice of the government. The approximate comparative data for the Arab world in Table 12 illustrates the importance of the different media, in one part of the 'Third World'.

TABLE 12. *Mass communications in the Middle East and North Africa, mid-1967**

Estimated circulation of daily newspapers	1,500,000
Estimated number of television sets	1,000,000
Estimated number of radio sets	7,000,000

Even these figures understate the importance of radio and television sets, because while the press figures refer to circulation, i.e. estimated number of readers, rather than copies sold, the radios and television sets reach a much wider public even amongst the poorest groups, since every café has one.

*Data compiled from Orbis Yearbook and National Publications.

There are two problems associated with radio and television facilities from our point of view: (*a*) there will often be many different broadcasting services and associated facilities, and (*b*) they are particularly difficult to seize. In some countries, where the internal security position is precarious, the governmental radio is heavily guarded, but even where this is not the case, these facilities are difficult to seize because their staff have a uniquely extensive way of raising the alarm. As for the duplication of broadcasting facilities, even Haiti, a very small and extremely backward country, has eighteen different radio stations, controlled by independent networks. Our objective is not merely to control but also to monopolize the flow of information, and we must therefore deal with every single facility. This would be difficult (and would also lead to a dispersal of our forces) if we tried to seize and hold every facility. Our strategy will therefore be to seize and hold just one facility, the one most closely associated with the voice of authority, while neutralizing the others. This is best done with the cooperation of some technical member of their staff who would be able to sabotage the facility from the inside. A single cooperative technician will be able temporarily to put out of action a radio station which would otherwise require a full-scale assault team.

If we are unable to recruit an internal saboteur, the next best alternative will be external sabotage. There is no need to cause any extensive damage since it will usually be possible to remove or destroy a small but essential part of the transmitter(s), thus effectively neutralizing the facility. The one broadcasting facility which we do have to seize and hold will present a special problem: on the one hand, our need for the facility is absolute; on the other, because it is such an obvious target, the governmental forces will certainly try to recapture it. This means that the team assigned to this target will have to be adequately staffed and equipped, and in order to obviate the need for the cooperation of the facility's personnel, should also include a skeleton technical staff. (Appendix B, on the military aspects of the *coup*, deals *inter alia* with the composition of the various teams.)

Telecommunications

Technical progress has evolved in our favour, since all the communication requirements between our own teams can be carried out by the cheap and reliable two-way transistor radios now universally available. We must, however, deny the opposition the use of their fixed communication systems, because by so doing we will paralyse their reaction and prevent them from deploying against us such forces as they still control. As Figure 3 shows, the neutralization of the telecommunication facilities will be complicated by their multiplicity, and it will be essential to achieve full coverage. The Left Socialist Revolutionary *coup* against the Bolsheviks in July 1918 failed partly because it failed to comprehend the need for a monopoly of *all* telecommunications. The Left Socialist Revolutionaries had infiltrated a group of the Cheka, the main instrument of Bolshevik power, and various army detachments; with these they arrested the head of the Cheka, Dzerzhinsky, seized many public buildings and the Moscow telegraph office. They failed, however, to seize the Telephone Office as well, and while they were sending cables all over Russia asking for generalized political support, Lenin used the telephone service to mobilize his fighting forces, and with these the *coup* was quickly crushed.

Internal security authorities are aware of the need for efficient communications, and apart from the facilities illustrated in the diagram on p. 121, there may also be independent networks for the exclusive use of the security forces. The French *gendarmerie* has a system of regional links which by-passes the public telephone and cable wires, and even in smaller countries, such as Ghana, the police can have a fully independent system (Table 13).

TABLE 13. *Police Telecommunication Facilities in Ghana*

---

63 fixed wireless stations, both high frequency and VHF radio telephones
6 dual-purpose mobile radio stations
Numerous man-portable radio sets

---

3. TELECOMMUNICATION FACILITIES AVAILABLE TO GOVERNMENT

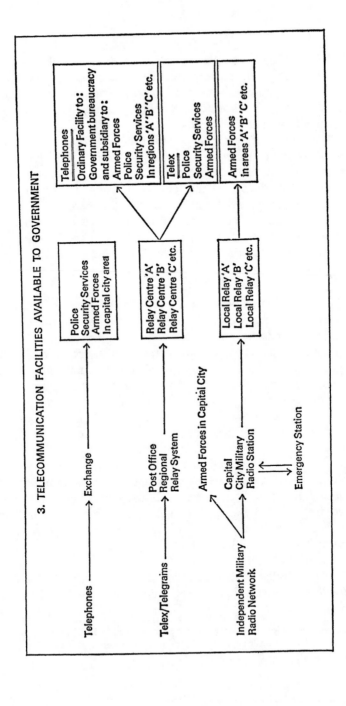

Telephones ──→ Exchange ──→ Police / Security Services / Armed Forces / In capital city area ──→ Relay Centre 'A' / Relay Centre 'B' / Relay Centre 'C' etc.

Post Office Regional Relay System

Telex/Telegrams ──→ Armed Forces in Capital City ──→ Local Relay 'A' / Local Relay 'B' / Local Relay 'C' etc.

Independent Military Radio Network ──→ Capital City Military Radio Station ⇄ Emergency Station

Telephones
────────
Ordinary Facility to:
Government bureaucracy
and subsidiary to:
Armed Forces
Police
Security Services
In regions 'A' 'B' 'C' etc.

Telex
────
Police
Security Services
Armed Forces

Armed Forces
in areas 'A' 'B' 'C' etc.

In the USA there are no national police networks, but the Department of Defense maintains a nation-wide and international system which is the largest single network in the world and which connects every US military installation with every other throughout the world.

We cannot, of course, hope to seize every two-way set in the hands of the police and the military authorities, but we should neutralize, by external or internal sabotage,* those facilities which can be identified and located. There is no need to seize and hold any of these facilities, and it will therefore be a matter of penetrating the central organization of each communication system for the brief period required to sabotage its operation though, again, *internal* sabotage will be easier and safer.

City Entry–Exit Road Links

During the active phase of the *coup* the unexpected arrival of even a small contingent of loyalist or uninfiltrated forces could seriously endanger our whole effort. When a government discovers that troops of its own armed forces are taking part in a *coup* in the capital city, its logical reaction may be to call on troops stationed elsewhere, in the hope that the infiltration of the armed forces is limited to those in the capital city. As it is not easy to infiltrate forces in the entire national territory, the government's hope may not be unfounded. We will attack the mechanism which could lead to the arrival of the loyalist troops in the capital city at each separate level: we will arrest those who would call them in, we will disrupt the telecommunications needed to reach them and we will also try to isolate identified loyalist forces by direct (though purely defensive) military means. We must also prevent the intervention of these forces by controlling the last level: the perimeter of the capital city and scene of the *coup*.

If the loyalist forces are to intervene in time, they will have to move rapidly and this will require the use of either the major

---

*The normal way of neutralizing an electrically-powered facility is to detonate small plastic charges on the grouped wire links between the facility and the public power supply (and independent generators, if any). These are usually not difficult to reach from the outside.

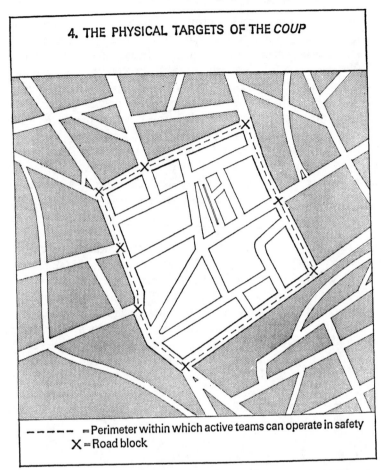

4. THE PHYSICAL TARGETS OF THE *COUP*

– – – – = Perimeter within which active teams can operate in safety
X = Road block

roads or alternatively air transport. If we can set up efficient
defensive road blocks at the appropriate places we should be able
to deny their entry into the capital city for the short period
required, that is, until we have established ourselves as the
government and received the allegiance of the bulk of the state
bureaucracy and military forces. Thus, by the time the forces of
intervention have reached the scene of the action, *they* will be
the isolated band of rebels. The most suitable places to block a
road with a small number of men and limited equipment, as well

as the techniques and implication of such actions, are discussed
in Appendix B and also in Chapter 5 where we deal with the
direct neutralization of the identified loyalist forces. Figure 4
illustrates the locations which would be chosen in a particular
(synthetic) example. But our control of the physical access to the
capital city will also serve other purposes. It will be one of the
ways in which we will establish the physical presence of the
new regime, and it will also allow us to prevent the escape of
governmental leaders and other personalities which we have
been unable to arrest. One of the dangers which we will face will
be the revitalization of counter-*coup* opposition, which could
result if a major governmental figure escapes from the capital
city and joins loyalist elements outside it. After all the efforts we
have made to neutralize such forces by internal means and by
interference with their transport and communications, our whole
work could be endangered. The loyalist forces could fail to reach
the capital but the political leadership could reach *them*. The
means at our disposal will not be sufficient to seal hermetically
the entire capital city, though of course much will depend on its
location and spatial spread. Brasilia, though open on all sides,
would be easy to seal off simply by closing the airport, since the
surface links are inadequate to allow rapid movement to the rest
of the country. Helsinki, on the other hand, would be spatially
convenient because, though not remote from the rest of the
country, it is surrounded by sea and lake so that a small number
of road blocks would effectively seal it.

Focal Traffic Points

The sight of tanks in the main squares of the capital city has
become a symbol of the *coup*,* but is also an expression of a
very real practical requirement: the need to establish a physical
presence in the centre of political activity. Every capital city has
an area which is the local equivalent of Whitehall in the UK or
Capitol Hill in the USA, in or near which the main political-
administrative facilities are concentrated. We will select and

*Tanks in the main squares are a feature of the Middle Eastern and Latin
American, but not of the African, military *coup*. Most African armies do not
in fact have tanks.

defend certain positions around and within this area and by so doing we will achieve a variety of purposes: (*a*) the positions will form a ring round the main area within which our active teams will operate so as to protect them from any hostile forces which may have penetrated the capital city; (*b*) they will assist in establishing our authority by giving visual evidence of our power; (*c*) they will filter movement to and from the area, thus enabling us to capture those whom we have been unable to arrest directly.

In order to achieve these different objectives, our blocking positions must be individually strong, since otherwise they may tempt any extant loyalist forces into a counter-attack. In any case, unless adequately staffed they will be unable to act as efficient filters to individual movements. We must therefore resist the temptation to secure every important location by blocking positions which are individually weak. As only a few of the possible locations will, in fact, be covered, it is essential to select them with special care. Focal traffic points will be easier to select in a coastal or riverine city, where a definite shape has been imposed to the capital city, and to the traffic flows within it. This is illustrated by Figure 5. In each particular case, the area which is the centre of political and bureaucratic activity will be well known to the local inhabitants, and it will therefore be a matter of selecting a perimeter of straight and fairly broad streets at the intersection of which we will establish our blocking positions. (The avenues and boulevards of Paris are ideal from this point of view.)

Airports and Other Transport Facilities

One of the classic moves in the period immediately following the *coup* is the closure of airports and the cancellation of all flights. This is part of the general tactic which aims at 'freezing' the situation by preventing the uncontrolled flow of people and information. There will also be other, more specific objectives: by closing the airport we will prevent the escape of those governmental leaders whom we have been unable to arrest. We will also prevent any inflow of loyalist forces into the area of the capital city. Because of the short time-span in which the *coup* takes

5. PHYSICAL TARGETS IN COASTAL CITY

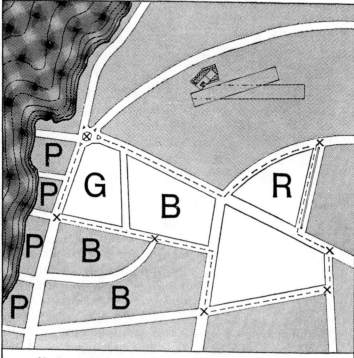

X = Road blocks at focal traffic points and city entry points

P = Densely populated sea-front district

B = Mixed residential areas

G = Governmental administrative and other public buildings

R = Governmental leaders residences

- - - - = Perimeter within which active teams can operate in safety place, air transport will be of very great importance; either we or the government could tip the balance of forces by flying in quite small contingents of our respective supporters. The size of the forces which can be moved by air may well be very small, but in the context of the delicate balance of the active phase of the *coup*, they could still play a decisive role.

Air transport is, however, very vulnerable insofar as it still relies on long and uninterrupted landing strips; therefore, if at all possible, we should avoid having to rely on it. To the extent that we are independent of support arriving by air, we should *therefore* prevent the use of all airfields in and around the area of the capital city. Some of these airfields will be military ones, but even if they are not they may still be heavily guarded. This could be a serious obstacle if the government still controls significant military forces outside the capital city and if transport planes are available to bring them into it. Seizing a defended air-field will certainly be difficult, but denying the use of one is very easy. A few vehicles parked on the runway, either by covert means or by a little cooperation from the inside, and 'covered' by a small fire-team to prevent them from being moved, will suffice to neutralize an entire airport. A few warning shots from suitable positions could also prevent any landings taking place.

Other organized forms of transport will only rarely be important in modern conditions. In many undeveloped countries railways play a very marginal role in the transport structure. Even where they are important economically, they will often be removed from the main population centres, having been built to connect mines and plantations with deep sea ports, as part of the colonial export economy rather than as links between the main population centres. In Europe and those parts of Latin America where this is not the case, railways will still be unimportant from our point of view because of the time element. In any case railways are extremely easy to neutralize. In the 1926 *coup* in Poland staged by Pilsudski, a great deal of the action revolved around the railway system but rail-borne troops never arrived in time to decide the issue, because both sides found it easy to prevent the other's movements, though not to ensure

their own. Where, as in Ethiopia, the railways are important –
or rather the single Addis Ababa–Djibouti railway line is important* – technical neutralization should be used. Railways rely
on a technical chain system *par excellence* and if a single section
of rail or signals is sabotaged, the whole system will temporarily
stop. The gap between two sections of rail is easily crossed, but
probably there will be no rolling stock on the other side.

Public Buildings

The need to provide the bureaucracy and the masses with visual
evidence of the reality and power of the *coup* is one of the
continuing elements in our analysis. Otherwise, this will be the
least defined and coherent of our groups of targets. The buildings which we will have to seize, in every case, will be the residence of those government leaders whom we have selected for
arrest, and those buildings which house facilities that we require,
such as the radio-television building. In the first case it will be a
matter of a brief penetration to achieve capture or arrest; in the
second, however, we will have to seize and occupy the building,
and perhaps resist attempts made to recapture it. But there will
be other official buildings which we will also have to occupy, or
at any rate control the access to. Those can only be loosely
defined as those buildings whose possession is associated with
the possession of political power.

Most countries have some form of elected assembly, a
parliament or its local equivalent, but in many of them political
power emanates from the palace of the president or other ruler
(or the central committee of the party); we should not be
deceived by constitutional fictions, and after spending so much
effort distinguishing between effective political power and its
symbols, we will not make the mistake of using our scarce
resources on the latter.

Nevertheless, there will be certain symbolic buildings which
could play an important role in the crucial transitional phase of
the *coup*: their possession by one side or the other will act as a
signal to the masses and the rank and file of the bureaucracy in

---

*A significant part of the Ethiopian army which is not fighting the
Somali *shiftas* is stationed in garrison towns along the single railway to the
sea.

the confused period when it is unclear which side is in control. Our possession of those symbols will then give us the allegiance of those who were waiting to choose one side or the other. Thus, though useless in direct material terms, it may well be worth while to seize those buildings which have a powerful symbolic value. In the Ghana *coup* of 1966 which brought down the N'krumah regime the very efficient and practical-minded leaders of the *coup* felt it necessary to fight their way into the presidential residence, Flagstaff House, though it contained neither N'krumah himself nor any important technical facilities. They realized that though it was an empty symbol *par excellence*, its possession was essential to secure the support of the Accra masses who naturally associated the control of political power with that particular building. Fortunately, by the very nature of such symbols there will be one, or at most, two such symbolic buildings whose possession will be an essential requirement.

Apart from the purely symbolic buildings, there will be others whose possession is highly desirable. These are the administrative headquarters of the army, police and security services. Thus in each case this group of targets will include the following:

(*a*) *The seat of effective political power*. This could be the Royal or Presidential palace or the building of the elected assembly or of the party Presidium or Central Committee;

(*b*) *The main administrative buildings*. The Ministry of Defence, the Ministry of the Interior, police and military headquarters, if separate;

(*c*) *Symbolic buildings*. Often the appropriate building will fall into one or other of the classifications above; where, however, there is a 'cultural' lag between the development of the country's political life and the traditional attitudes, the masses will still associate political power with an 'obsolete' building.

The *coup* will be practically over (in its 'active' phase) by the time the citizenry wakes up and starts to investigate the possession of buildings symbolic or otherwise. We can therefore postpone the occupation of some of these targets to the later stages. Since in direct practical terms other targets will be more important, or at any rate more urgent, the best way of dealing with the symbolic and administrative targets will be to use them as assembly points for those teams which have already completed their primary mission.

Neutralizing the Political Forces II: particular groups

Which organized groups will be sufficiently strong to oppose us even if the voice of the government is silent and the capital city visibly in our hands? Not many, but we must remember that even one well-organized demonstration, or a well-timed strike, could pose a serious threat to the *coup* in the delicate transitional phase. It is therefore essential to identify such groups and, once identified, to neutralize them before the *coup*. Once it is known that a *coup* has taken place, the leaders of the militant organization(s) concerned will immediately prepare for action; they themselves will then be more difficult to arrest and their organizations will be halfway underground.

In countries where political conflict is limited to the verbal dimension, this kind of dramatic and rapid response to political change will be unknown; but elsewhere, where political conflicts can be violent and where all organized forces, whether primarily political or not, can be drawn into them, this type of response is more or less automatic. Political parties in the Middle East and South America, trade-union movements in southern Europe, religious movements in South Vietnam have little in common except (*a*) their ability to respond in this way and (*b*) that even without the weaponry that some of them have, they could be a real threat to the *coup*. We will conduct our analysis in terms of those three types of 'political force' because their features will largely subsume those of other kinds of organized groups, which may be relevant in particular countries. In the United States or Britain, for example, where neither trade unions nor religious groups nor political parties are sufficiently militant to oppose a *coup* after it has seized its initial targets, the groups which may have this capability (such as para-military movements of the paranoid right) will be organized in a manner which includes features of all three.

One of the points which we must bear in mind is that not all the organized groups which are important in normal political life will also be important in the highly restricted and spasmodic politics of the *coup*. Conversely, groups which in ordinary political life are of very limited importance could emerge as real threats. If, for example, we failed to neutralize the organization of, say, the National Rifle Association in the USA, or the National Union of Students in the UK, their reaction – however ineffectual *per se* – could still endanger the *coup* by slowing down the process of political stabilization in as much as they could provoke conflicts which would re-open the whole issue. Other, more prudent, groups would then re-examine the possibility of challenging our position, while the use of violence to stop the agitation of the groups we have overlooked could lead to further opposition since the side-effects of violence would increase the awareness of and hostility to the *coup*.

Finally, there are certain political forces which must *not* be neutralized (apart from those groups which have agreed to support us). These are those groups which are generally regarded as extremist but whose effective powers are limited. By allowing them a certain freedom of action we will give them an opportunity to oppose us, and their opposition will have two favourable by-products: (*a*) we will be able to gain the support of those political forces which fear *them* more than us; (*b*) we will be able to step forward and fight *other* groups after having associated them with the extremists in question. This can, however, be a dangerous game to play; in the confused and dramatic situation of the *coup*, the extremists could gain in power and political support, and it is therefore possible that the time which we have allowed them to discredit the opposition will work in their favour.

RELIGIOUS ORGANIZATIONS

In many economically developed countries religious organizations no longer have much political power, though they may still be an important social force. The leaders of religious groups can be influential in social and, to a degree, political life, but the allegiance of the believers is rarely expressed by direct and forceful action in the political field. In economically backward countries, and in those whose development is limited or very recent, it is otherwise. Where the newer technology of man has only been recently applied, or not at all, the older technology of God is still of paramount importance. This can be a source of very considerable political power to the organizations which are identified with the appropriate beliefs and which are able to channel the sentiments of the believers. Leaving aside local cults, which are too fragmented to be important in terms of national politics, and which in any case tend to be apolitical,* we see that even universal religions will differ in their degree of political involvement.

The role of the Catholic Church in Italy since the war illustrates the power which can be accumulated by a well-organized religious group, even when operating in circumstances which are unfavourable from the *religious* point of view. Though most male Italians seldom or never go to church, Italian women are keen and regular churchgoers. Italy being a democratic country where women have the vote, it is obvious that if the organized Church is willing to direct its followers to vote for a particular party, that party will gain the bulk of the women's vote before it even opens its electoral campaigns. The Church has generally been willing to give such specific directions, and one particular party has benefited: the *Democrazia Cristiana* (DC). Aided by its assured majority of the female vote, the DC has ruled Italy, alone or in various coalitions, since 1946, and it has done so largely because of the support received from the Church. It is hardly surprising therefore that the Church has been able to dominate the DC and that, through the DC, it has influenced every aspect of Italian national life.

This is no vague influence exercised on a plane of generalized authority, but rather a constant supervision of political activity, conducted at the provincial level by the bishops and at the national level by the Pope and his associates. At each level of the state bureaucracy the Church, directly or indirectly, exercises its influence: on civil-service jobs and promotions; on the allocation of investment funds and of the various kinds of government grants; on administrative decisions dealing with 'zoning' and

---

*Local cults may be important from the point of view of the local administration, but not in terms of national politics.

building regulations. This influence has brought its rewards. While the facilities of the state bureaucracy have steadily deteriorated compared with the dynamic private and semi-state sector, the Church's educational and religious facilities have steadily expanded; money to build and the permissions required to do so have never been lacking.

If we failed to neutralize the organization of the Church in Italy, it could inspire and co-ordinate opposition to us through its capillary network of parish churches. Parishioners are used to hearing political messages from the pulpit;* priests are used to receiving detailed political briefs from their bishop and the latter receive their instructions from the Vatican. Our neutralization of the telecommunications facilities will not prevent the flow of instructions: the Vatican maintains its own radio station and this could be used to contact directly the organization throughout the country.

The Catholic Church plays a similar role in certain other countries, where it has a 99·9 per cent nominal membership and the status of the national religion, but the stronger state structure of Spain and Portugal, let alone France, has denied it the pre-eminent position it has in Italy. The intervention of the Church would, however, be a powerful factor in much of the Catholic world, including South America, especially if the motive force behind the *coup* was identified as being anti-clerical.

Islam, which has the comprehensive nature of a religion, a political system and a civilization, is still (though much decayed) a major political force and its leaders play a recognized political role. The 'doctors' of El Azhar University in Cairo, one of the main theological institutions of the Muslim world, are periodically prompted by the Nasir regime into openly political declarations; no single leader in Islam has the authority of a Pope because the system is less centralized, but in each country the local leaders are still very important. Even the spread of 'Arab Socialism' has not impaired the position of Islam, and govern-

---

*In a recent and very successful Italian film, the parish priest was shown explaining to his flock that he did not want to give them a pre-election brief, but he merely asked them to vote for a party which was Democratic and which was Christian, '. . . *Democratico e Cristiano, Cristiano e Democratico. . .*'

ments which follow an extreme left 'line' in all foreign and some domestic matters are still unwilling (or unable) to challenge the status of Islam as the state religion. When such a course was tentatively suggested by an obscure member of the present Syrian government, the leadership (which follows an almost Peking 'line' in all other fields) was forced to denounce him officially. Whether this resilience means that the Islamic leadership of particular countries could act as an *active* political force is another matter. The structures of Islam as an organized religion are fossilized; the fluid and dynamic aspect of the movement in its early days has been replaced by a dogmatic and extremely conservative set of beliefs, whose inflexibility is one of the causes of the present travail of the Arab world.

The political sterility of Islam in recent times has meant that, though it has been used by governments to propagate *their* political initiatives, Islam *per se* has only acted when a direct attack has been made on religious orthodoxy.* Consequently, unless our *coup* has a definite anti-Islamic colouring, religious leaders in Muslim countries will not initiate any action against us. We must therefore prevent our opponents imposing such a colouring on our *coup*.

In the intermittent political warfare between 'Arab-Socialists' and the monarchies, while the latter are accused of being 'tools of the "Zionist-imperialist oil monopolies"', the former are accused of wanting to eradicate Islam with their godless beliefs. Actually even the *soi-disant* 'progressives' would not dream of challenging Islam, which is after all the main factor – through the language of the Koran – which binds the Arab countries, separated as they are by both history and geography.

Thus, with the one qualification made above, we can ignore Islam as an active political force. The same goes for Hinduism which, though otherwise very different, shares the passive political role of Islam. Though some political forces in India have successively made use of Hindu sentiments, religious leaders as

*This and subsequent statements about Islam and the Arab world refer to Sunni Islam: the heretical Shi's sects and their offshoots are a different matter. Their political and religious leadership is often embodied in the same person, and they are often politically very active.

such have never actually initiated any major political action.
(Even the periodic agitation against cow slaughter is instigated
by the extreme right parties.)

An extreme example of the potentialities of a dynamic
religious leadership is the 'main line' Buddhist movement in
South Vietnam. The almost continual warfare of the last generation and the politically destructive effect of the Diem regime have
led to a collapse of the social and political structures of the
country, while its economy has been reduced to localized subsistence agriculture, allied with urban dependence on US aid.
In this situation the newer economic, political and social forces
have become extremely weak and the groups based on the older
religious affiliations have emerged as the only valid civilian
forces in Vietnamese society. Apart from the main line Buddhist
movement, led by Thich Tri Quang and other regional leaders,
there is the following alignment of forces (early 1968):

Hoa Hao: a reformed Buddhist group with a large following
in the southern (Delta) part of the country. Their leadership is
politically orientated and, except for strictly local alliances, is
anti-Viet Cong. They appear to have built up the rudiments of
an armed militia.

Cao Dai: an important Buddhist sect which has a history of
political participation.

Binh Xuyen: a small but very active part-sect and part-secret
society. Its main area of strength is in the Saigon region, and
before the Diem regime displaced them, the Binh Xuyen used
to 'own' the city's police force – and its underworld. The sect
has been influenced by the Chinese secret societies from across
the river in Cholon, and the effect of repression at the hands of
Diem has been to drive it underground rather than to destroy it.

Catholics: until Diem's fall, the large Catholic minority was
able to dominate the Buddhist majority. Many of the South
Vietnamese community are refugees from the North; under the
French many Catholics cooperated actively with the colonial
power and served in the French armed forces. Now that the
South appears to be going the way the North went in 1954, the
community has reached a desperate *impasse*. Their activity

against a pro-Viet Cong (or just pro-peace) *coup* would be immediate and probably very effective.

All these religious groups could intervene against a *coup*: their meeting places could be used to assemble and shelter our opponents; the priesthood could inspire and coordinate mass agitation against us; finally, their direct influence on the army and the bureaucratic rank-and-file could be used to resist the imposition of our authority.

The religious groups which can be important in particular countries will differ doctrinally, but will be organizationally sufficiently similar to adopt a general method of neutralization. If they operate private broadcasting facilities, such as the Vatican Radio or the small radio stations of American missionary sects in many parts of the world, we will put them temporarily out of action. Religious meeting places should not be closed by administrative methods, which are liable to foment rather than stifle opposition, but access to them should be barred by 'incidental' roadblocks.

The leadership of religious organizations presents a special problem in terms of neutralization: because of their particular psychological role in the minds of public opinion it will usually be extremely unwise to arrest the actual hierarchic leadership. Fortunately, the actual decision-makers within religious organizations will often be younger men who are not in the public eye but who are the key figures from our point of view. If the real decision-makers are not also the hierarchical leaders, we will arrest them; but if the two roles are embodied in the same person or persons, we will not do so. In concrete terms, a Thich Tri Quang, who is an effective decision-maker, but not formally in the higher leadership, can (and should) be arrested; but a Pope, who is both the representational and the effective leader, cannot however be arrested without stimulating a great deal of opposition the impact of which will outweigh any advantage to be gained from the arrest.

POLITICAL PARTIES

Unlike the other groups which constitute a potential source of
opposition to the *coup*, political parties are our direct competitors,
in the sense that their primary purpose – like our own – is the
accumulation of political power.* This will not necessarily make
them the main, or even a significant, potential threat to us, but
it will mean that their response to the *coup* will be particularly
prompt. Whether this response will be verbal and purely
declaratory, or whether it will be more direct and effective, will
depend on a variety of factors, including the nature of their
leadership, organization and membership. Because political
parties are as diverse as the countries within which they compete
for power, we will classify them in certain categories as a prelude
to examining the methods of their individual neutralization.

'Machine' Parties

Where politics is a business like any other, parties take the form
of an association whose purpose is the procurement of votes in
exchange for specific and material rewards. The local 'boss'
secures votes for the party at election time in exchange for cash
and/or bureaucratic jobs for himself or his nominees. The
deputies in the Assembly then deliver their votes to the government in exchange for definite favours, some of which are retained
and some of which are passed down to those who secured their
election. The 'machine' party can flourish in societies as different as early twentieth-century America, Egypt between the
wars and present-day South America. It needs two main ingredients: an elective parliamentary democracy and a socially
backward electorate. In the United States at the beginning of the
century the immigrant communities were largely composed of
eastern and southern Europeans, whose mother-countries were
economically, and often politically, unsophisticated. Thus the
newly-arrived immigrant lacked the political awareness required
to obtain direct concessions from the government, in the shape
of social welfare legislation or labour codes. He soon learnt,
however, to obtain indirect favours by promising his support to

*This is their *purpose*. Their *function*, however, is to aggregate interests.

the local ward organization of the party – i.e. if the votes were delivered on election day and the candidate elected, rewards would eventually be received in return. Present-day 'machine' parties, such as the *Democrazia Cristiana* in parts of Italy, *Acción Democrática* in Venezuela, and MNR in Bolivia, do not distribute their rewards as widely as the old municipal machines in the United States. This is because these parties participate in the *empleocracia,* which dominates political societies in which industry and commerce are undeveloped and agriculture the monopoly of peasant subsistence farmers or aristocratic land-lords. In these conditions politics and the associated jobs in the state bureaucracy are the main avenues of middle-class enterprise, and the party is the framework (together with legal training) for the middle-class activity of office-hunting.

Machine parties have their rationale in the contrast between the constitutional structures and the social ones in countries which are both poor and 'democratic'. Their whole manner of operation revolves around the exchange of votes for rewards at every level; in other words it requires the functioning of the parliamentary apparatus, with its periodic elections. In the event of a *coup* this institutional framework would be frozen and the machine made powerless. Even if the machine has a base of mass support, its leadership, being a coalition of local power structures without a national 'presence', will not be able to mobilize it. We will therefore ignore the 'machine' parties and will not need to take any particular action in their regard.

'*Insurrectional*' *Parties*★

Such parties may or may not participate in open political life (if it exists in our target country) but the primary purpose of insurrectional parties is to destroy the system rather than to work it. Like the Bolshevik party before 1917, the Muslim Brotherhood in Egypt, Communist and extreme right-wing parties in many parts of the world, these parties live a semi-legal existence, with a cellular organization, an 'underground' mentality and, frequently a para-military element. Such parties

★The alternative term, 'revolutionary parties' has left-wing connotations, while insurrection covers both extremes of the spectrum.

are characterized by their adherence to a set of definite ideological beliefs, a rigidly centralized organization and their preoccupation with the use of direct methods to achieve political ends.

In the social and economic conditions of Western Europe and North America, insurrectional parties are numerically weak and their challenge to the system is usually conducted in an atmosphere of unreality, though from time to time they can gather a mass following among certain sectors of the population which are outside the mainstream of national life. The 'Black Power' movement in the United States, for example, has all the traits of an insurrectional party, but it only operates amongst the Negro communities in the ghettoes whose social and economic conditions are those of an economically backward society. In the 'Third World', however, the constant pressure of economic deprivation can generate a revolutionary mentality amongst wide sections of the population, which insurrectional parties try to channel and exploit. Their organization, however, is often inadequate to the task and much of the endemic guerrilla activity in Latin America and the insurgencies in South-East Asia are outside their control.

Insurrectional parties can oppose us in three main ways: (a) through the agitation of the masses, to the extent that they have a mass following; (b) by direct means, such as assassination and sabotage; (c) by syndicalist agitation. Insurrectional parties usually have an authoritarian leadership structure and much of their strength, in the confused circumstances which would follow a *coup*, would derive from the coherence of a centralized leadership. We should therefore make every effort to identify and 'isolate' their key decision-makers. The emphasis on party discipline and the habit of waiting for 'directives' from the higher leadership render many insurrectional parties powerless once the leadership has ceased to function. Though the social pressures which are the sources of strength of an insurrectional party may lead to its revival, this will not take place in the short period of time which concerns us. This vulnerability of insurrectional parties was strikingly demonstrated in the case of the Muslim Brotherhood, *Al-Ikhwan al-Muslimun*. The *Ikhwan* was a major force in Egyptian political life after the war, and its large mass following, its network of economic and educational activities and its para-military youth groups gave it a great deal of direct power. Its effectiveness, however, derived largely from the coherent leadership of its founder, Shaykh Hasan al-Banna, and the movement rapidly declined after his death (in unexplained circumstances) just after the failed *coup* of late 1948. Where necessary, therefore, the committee or personal leadership of the insurrectional party should be arrested and held in isolation for the duration of the *coup*. Because of the emphasis on party discipline, the beheaded movement will probably abstain from action in the short but critical period following our seizure of power.

Para-Bureaucratic Parties

In one-party states, such as those of Communist countries, much of Africa, and Mexico, the party has lost its major role: the competition for the allegiance of the masses. Being in a position of monopoly, the party is also in danger of appearing superfluous. But, like any other bureaucratic organization, the party can survive the loss of its primary function, either as a system of spoliation or as an ancillary or supervisor of the administrative bureaucracy of the state. African parties, formed during the political struggles which preceded independence, have often legislated for their monopoly of power as soon as they have attained it. Some, like TANU (Tanzanian African National Union), have turned into constructive galvanizers of the communal and state development programmes; others, like N'krumah's old party in Ghana, became adjuncts to the personal leadership and a system of outdoor relief for his 'activist' followers. The majority, however (until swept away by the military dictatorships), have acted as the principal agent in the main local industry: politics.

The para-bureaucratic party treats the state bureaucracy as its subordinate. It investigates its activities, reports on its behaviour to the higher leadership, and often demands special privileges and concessions. These parties do not have a mass following except within the framework of normal political life, when they can be relied upon to produce demonstrations *for* this or that stand of the leadership. As soon as the hold of the leadership is threatened, as soon as the police apparatus no longer acts as its 'muscle', the para-bureaucratic party dissolves. We can therefore ignore it in the active stage of the *coup*. However, its secondary function, intelligence and security, will be important and will be dealt with as part of our general defensive measures towards such organizations.

Parties in Developed Countries

Whether it is a two-party system, as in much of the Anglo-Saxon world where parties are in effect coalitions of pressure groups, or whether they are the class- or religion-based parties of much of continental Europe, the major political parties in developed and democratic countries will not present a direct threat to the *coup*. Though such parties have mass support at election time, neither they nor their followers are versed in the techniques of mass agitation. The comparative stability of political life has deprived them of the experience required to employ direct methods, and the whole climate of their operation revolves around the concept of periodic elections. Even where, as in France and Italy, there are large and nominally revolutionary parties, two or more decades of parliamentary life have reduced their affinity with revolutionary methods.

The apparatus of the party, with its branches and local organizers, can, however, allow them to perform a role of information and co-ordination which could be potentially dangerous. Even though their leadership may not take any action, the apparatus can still serve as the framework for anti-*coup* agitation. We will therefore close – administratively – the network of branches, and this should be sufficient to neutralize this particular threat.

The only serious threat from this direction will come from the trade-union movements which are affiliated to the mass parties of the Left. Their experience of industrial agitation has provided a natural training for mass intervention against a *coup*, but this will be dealt with separately below.

TRADE UNIONS

Wherever there is a significant degree of industrial development, and in many countries where there is not, trade unions are a major political force. Because of their experience of industrial agitation, which can be readily applied to political purposes, the response of trade unions to the *coup* could constitute a serious danger to us. The mass following of trade unions – unlike that of political parties – is in continuous session: polling booths are only open once every five years, but factories work all the year round. The immediacy of the threat presented by trade unions will depend on their size, cohesion and degree of militancy: the fragmented syndicalism of Britain, with its purely electoral politics, would not, for example, add up to the threat of, say, the Italian movement with its centralization and long history of political strikes.

The experience of Bolivia since the 1952 Revolution illustrates how a single trade union and its activities can dominate a country's political life. Bolivia is one of the poorest countries of South America, whose economy is characterized by subsistence farming and the activities of the large tin industry. Before the Revolution and the nationalization of the mines owned by the Patino, Aramayo and Hochschild interests, the miners had worked in physical and economic conditions of extreme harshness. Following their emancipation, they naturally wanted to achieve immediate and substantial improvements in these conditions and COMIBOL, the state tin-mining organization, started immediate reforms.

It was soon discovered, however, that the geological and economic conditions of the industry required an increase in productivity which could only be achieved by introducing much new machinery and reducing the labour force. As the only source of capital was the United States, the miners' leaders opposed the reforms on the dual plank of no *'yanqui'* capitalism and no redundancies. Such problems are familiar from nearer home, but the crucial difference was that the miners were also an *army*. They had been armed by the middle-class leaders of the revolutionary MNR (*Movimento Nacionalista Revolucionario*)

Party in order to act as a counter-weight to the old army dominated by associates of the mine-owners. The Revolution disbanded the army so that the miners could not only exert political
and economic pressures but could also use more direct, military
methods. Until the MNR leadership found a counter-weight in
the unions organized amongst the peasant farmers, the Indian
campesinos, who were also armed, the miners had things pretty
much their way. Led by militants of the *Catavi-Siglo Veinte*
mines, the miners imposed their control on COMIBOL, and
therefore on the country which depends on it as the only major
source of foreign exchange. Certainly no *coup* could have held
on to power without the miners' consent, and even if the central
institutions in La Paz could have been seized, the real power base
in the mines would still have been under the control of the union
leaders.

Even without the special circumstances which operate in
Bolivia, trade unions will often be a major political force,
especially in terms of the situation immediately following a *coup*.
But much will depend on the particular organizational structure
of the trade unions, and crucially on the degree of effective
centralization and the nature of their political affiliations. In
Britain, the main focus of decision-making within the trade-
union movement as a whole is the executive of individual unions,
but in some of them it has shifted to the shop floor. Apart
from this fragmentation, which would at least impair the speed
of reaction to a *coup*, the largely mainstream politics of British
labour would not be a suitable framework for direct measures.

In France and Italy, the trade-union movement is not divided
on craft lines, as in Britain, or on industrial lines, as in the
USA and much of northern Europe, but on political lines.
Individual industrial unions are affiliated to central organizations which are associated with particular parties. In both
countries the largest organization is controlled by the local
Communist party, with smaller Social-Democrat and Catholic
ones. The Communist organizations, CGL in Italy and
CGT in France,* both have a long experience of political

*Confédération Générale du Travail (CGT); *Confederazione Generale del*
Lavoro (CGL).

activism expressed in 'political' and 'general' strikes, pheno-
mena of almost purely historical significance in Anglo-Saxon
countries.*

Unless our *coup* is directly linked to the Communist party,
the central organizations of French and Italian trade unionism
would react to it, and do so in predictable ways. Immediately
after the *coup* they would: (a) try to establish contact with other
'democratic forces' to form a popular front opposition; (b)
contact their national network of branches to coordinate a
general strike; (c) put into execution their contingency plans for
'underground' activity and illegal survival. The only tactic
which would present a threat to us is the general strike, which
would be organized with the deliberate intention of 'confront-
ing' the forces of the *coup*. Our general measures would affect
the overall performance of this emergency programme, but
specific action would be needed as well in order to avoid the
confrontation which the unions would probably seek. Both the
CGT and the CGL have memories of the wartime resistance
movements: both are aware of the destabilizing nature of open
repression and they would therefore try to provoke us into using
violence.

Though some form of confrontation may be inevitable, it is
essential to avoid bloodshed, because this may well have crucial
negative repercussions amongst the personnel of the armed
forces and the police. The avoidance of bloodshed in tense
crowd situations is a matter of technique, and competent
handling of our incorporated armed and uniformed forces will be
essential.†

The incidents of Reggio Emilia in Italy in the summer of
1964 in which seven people died following a 'political' strike,

*Cf. the events of May 1968 in France.

†The renewal of political activism in recent years in both Britain and the
United States has intensified the search for effective means of controlling
mobs. The study of mass psychology and the development of assorted
gadgetry should not obscure the fundamental principles of mob control.
These are: (a) the need to keep the mob in open spaces so that claustro-
phobic and physical pressures are avoided, and (b) the need to break down the
anonymity of the individual in a mob by making *selective* arrests.

illustrated how an incompetent police force can impair the authority of the government it is trying to protect.*

If the trade unions of our target country approximate to Franco-Italian levels of political effectiveness it will be necessary – assuming that our *coup* is not politically linked with them – to identify and arrest their leaders and close their headquarters in order to impede the operation of their secondary leadership. Elsewhere, it will be a matter of orientating our general measures to deal with the particular threats which trade-union movement could prevent.

*Cf. the destabilizing effects of the behaviour of the police in Paris on the night of Friday 4 May 1968, which was the detonator of the crisis.

5. The Execution of the *Coup d'État*

'As soon as the moral power of national represen-
tation was destroyed, a legislative body, whatever
it might be, meant no more to the military than a
crowd of five hundred men, less vigorous and
disciplined than a battalion of the same number.'
Madame de Staël referring to Napoleon's coup
d'état

'I came in on a tank, and only a tank will evict
me.' *Abu Zuhair Yahya, Iraqui Prime Minister,
1968*

The active phase of a *coup* is like a military operation – only more
so. If the general principle of tactics is the application of force
at the right place, the *coup* achieves this with surgical precision
by striking at the organizational heart of the whole state; if
speed is often important in military operations, in the *coup* it is
an essential requirement. But the *coup* differs from most military
operations in one crucial respect: while in war it is often ad-
vantageous to retain some forces as reserves to be used in later
(and possibly more critical) phases of the conflict, in a *coup* the
principle of total commitment applies. The active stage takes
place in one short period of time and forces held back today will
be useless tomorrow: all our forces must therefore be used in the
one decisive engagement.

The fact that the *coup* has practically no time-dimension
means that we will rarely be able to correct errors made during
its execution; in war, tactics can be changed, weapons can be
replaced, plans re-shaped and men re-trained on the basis of
combat experience, but in the *coup* there will not be sufficient
time for any feed-back to operate. In this the *coup* is similar to
the most modern form of warfare, the strategic missile strike,
and the time factor places the entire burden of decision-making

in the planning stage. Every target must be studied in detail before the *coup*. The team assigned to seize it must match it in terms of size and composition; its every move must be planned in advance and no tactical flexibility can be allowed.

With this degree of detailed planning, there will be no need for any sort of headquarters structure in the active stage of the *coup*; for if there is no scope for decision-making there is no need for decision-makers and their apparatus. In fact, having a headquarters would be a serious disadvantage: it would constitute a concrete target for the opposition and one which would be both vulnerable and easily identified. As soon as the *coup* starts, the ruling group will know that something is happening, but unless *coups* are very frequent in the country, they will not know what that something is; it could be a mutiny, an insurrection, the opening of a guerrilla war, or even the beginning of an invasion by a foreign power. All these forms of conflict represent threats to the regime, but they are all different in terms of their immediate significance and – more important – in terms of the measures which are required to meet them. We should avoid taking any action that will clarify the nature of the threat and thus reduce the confusion that is left in the defensive apparatus of the regime. Our teams will emerge from their bases and proceed to seize their designated targets while operating as independent units; their collective purpose and their coordinations will thus remain unknown until it is too late for any effective opposition. The leaders of the *coup* will be scattered among the various teams, each joining the team whose ultimate target requires his presence; thus the spokesman of the *coup* will be with the team which will seize the radio-television station and the prospective chief of police will be with the team whose target is the police headquarters. As each team will be both small and highly mobile, and as there is no headquarters throughout the active phase of the *coup*, the opposition will not have any single target on which it will be able to concentrate its forces. In this way their numerical superiority will be dissipated and the smaller forces of the *coup* will have local superiority in the area of each particular target. This will be the key of the victory of the *coup*.

On the Eve

In the last two chapters we have surveyed the planning of the *coup* in terms of the neutralization of the 'professional' defences of the state, and the selection of those targets which will assist the neutralization of the 'political' forces. We analysed the structure of the armed forces and the other means of coercion, and we saw that much of the armed forces, a significant part of the police system, and some of the security services, could not intervene – either for or against us – in the event of a *coup*. This was due to their remote location, dispersed deployment, or because their training and equipment were inadequate – or over-specialized. Then we infiltrated the relatively small part of the apparatus which did have an intervention capability, so that much of it was technically neutralized and some of it totally subverted. This will ensure for us the neutrality of much of the defences of the state and the active cooperation of some of its parts. The infiltration of the army and police has given us an instrument: the units which we have incorporated and which form the forces of the *coup*. We have also prepared for the use of this instrument by selecting the targets on which it will be used: we have identified the physical targets which must be seized and those which will have to be sabotaged or otherwise interdicted; we have selected the leading personalities amongst the potential opposition, both in and out of the government, and prepared for their arrest.

But one major task, however, has not been covered in the planning stage: the forcible isolation of the 'hard-core' loyalist forces. Hopefully, the strength of those forces which we have been unable to infiltrate and which also have an intervention capability will not be very great. But even if they are weak in absolute terms, we dare not ignore them. To do so, would be to invalidate all the measures we have taken to insulate the capital city – and ourselves – from the intervention of hostile forces. The extreme instability of the balance of forces during the active phase of the *coup* means that what in other circumstances would only be a minor threat could then have disastrous consequences, and if the 'hard-core' loyalist forces are large in relation to our own, we will indeed have to divert much of our forces to their isolation.

Though we have been unable to penetrate these 'hard-core' loyalist forces, two things will probably have been achieved: (*a*) their number, quality and location will be known to us, and (*b*) our general measures of neutralization will have reduced their overall effectiveness. Their fighting capability will not have been eroded but, as Table 14 illustrates, their intervention against us will be delayed and disrupted.

Our purpose is not to destroy the loyalist forces militarily (since we will be able to deal with their cadres administratively after the *coup*) but merely to immobilize them for a few crucial hours. The tactics which will be used must be exclusively defensive: a ring of blocking positions around each concentration of loyalist forces or, if this is not possible, a similar ring around the capital city. Thus, though we will be on the strategic offensive (in the sense that we are the ones who want to change the situation in general) we will also be on the tactical defensive, and this will give us important technical and psychological advantages. By using defended roadblocks to isolate the loyalist forces, we will put the onus of initiating any fighting on them: our forces will be content to wait and it will be the loyalist forces which will try to pass through. Should a column of loyalist forces arrive at the roadblock, their leaders will be faced by opposite numbers wearing the same uniform, and belonging to the same corporate entity, perhaps even to the same regiment. Both sides will state that they are 'obeying orders', but interestingly enough, the 'orders' of the leaders of our forces will probably appear more legitimate than those of the leaders of the loyalist troops. Owing to our arrests and our interdiction of the physical facilities, the 'legitimate' orders will probably have taken an unusual form: the source of the orders to the loyalist troops will probably be somebody other than the appropriate superior in the hierarchy; the method used to convey them will probably be an unusual emergency one; *and the actual orders indistinguishable in form from ones which might have been issued by the planners of a* coup.

Thus the officers of the loyalist forces may have received orders stating, 'Move into the city centre, hold the Parliament building and the radio station.' The leadership may have added that they would be acting against the forces of a *coup* but, even so, such orders would have insurrectional undertones. When army officers find themselves doing unusual things, their natural reaction is to try and fit them into familiar patterns; the most familiar pattern of all will be to arrive at the conclusion that the 'politicians are guilty of yet another "mess" '. The most probable course of action will be to request clarification from their superior officers. It is to be hoped that these officers will have either decided to remain neutral, or else have been arrested; in either case the 'clarification' will never arrive.

If, on the other hand, the loyalist units decide to force the roadblock, we will benefit from the tactical advantages of the defensive. These include the opportunity of choosing the place (natural obstructions such as bridges and tunnels) and the opportunity of deploying and camouflaging weapons and men. In order to make the fullest use of both the psychological and the tactical advantages, the blocking position should have a dual structure: a (largely symbolic) first line composed of some suitable physical obstacle, such as cross-parked heavy vehicles, with a few men bearing 'orders' which forbid all passage; beyond this, there will be a second (military) line, much stronger numerically, with weapons and men deployed to repel an eventual assault (the operational detail involved is discussed in Appendix B). The defenders of the blocking position should inform the incoming loyalist forces that there is such a second line of defence: this should be partly camouflaged and would then serve as a deterrent even if it is numerically weak compared to the opposition, since its real strength will be difficult to ascertain.

The situation at the blocking position will require very delicate handling and it will be necessary that the soldiers on our side understand that their primary function is to avoid a conflict, rather than to engage in it successfully. In concrete terms, their mission will be a delaying operation rather than a decisive one and this will have precise implications in terms of the weapons and tactics to be employed.

TABLE 14. *The Mechanics of Intervention of the Loyalist Forces*

Phase	Effect of our general measures
1. Police/security agency personnel raise initial alarm and seek to contact their HQ.	Telephone exchange has been seized, telex cable links have been sabotaged, radio relays are shut off. They must therefore send a verbal message.
2. Police/security agency HQ verify the reports and realize the seriousness of the threat. HQ tries to communicate with political leadership.	As above for communications. Some messengers fail to arrive as focal traffic points are gradually occupied.
3. Political leadership calls for army and police intervention.	As above for communications. Some units missing from their barracks; others refuse to move; others cannot move because of technical neutralization.
4. Political leaders begin to realize the extent of our infiltration of the armed forces and police. Loyalist troops respond.	As above for communications. Only military radio links can be used to communicate with loyalist forces.
5. Uninfiltrated forces assemble and prepare for intervention. They try to reach political leadership for a confirmation of their orders. Some defect to us, others choose neutrality, but some remain under the control of the government.	Many political leaders no longer available; some arrested and some in hiding.
6. Loyalist forces move on to capital city or if already within its area, move in to the city centre.	Airports closed and landing strips interdicted. Railways interrupted and trains stopped. City entry points controlled by our roadblocks.

Loyalist forces in capital city area are then isolated by direct means

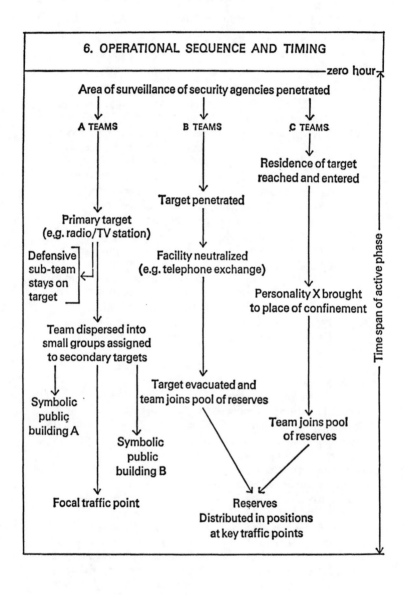

6. OPERATIONAL SEQUENCE AND TIMING

zero hour

Area of surveillance of security agencies penetrated

A TEAMS   B TEAMS   C TEAMS

Residence of target reached and entered

Target penetrated

Primary target (e.g. radio/TV station)

Defensive sub-team stays on target

Facility neutralized (e.g. telephone exchange)

Personality X brought to place of confinement

Team dispersed into small groups assigned to secondary targets

Symbolic public building A

Target evacuated and team joins pool of reserves

Team joins pool of reserves

Symbolic public building B

Focal traffic point

Reserves Distributed in positions at key traffic points

Time span of active phase

Timing, Sequence and Security

Ideally, the timing of the *coup* will be completely flexible so that we can take advantage of any favourable circumstances which may arise, such as the temporary absence of the leadership from the capital city or the outbreak of some coincidental civil disorders. This flexibility, which would be highly desirable, is only rarely possible because the infiltration of the army and police will be a dynamically unstable process: the circle of those who have decided to join us will grow and continue growing as a 'band-wagon' effect is generated; but unless the *coup* materializes, there will eventually be a movement into neutrality or even opposition. Meanwhile, the danger of denunciation will also increase as more and more people become aware that a *coup* is being planned, or at any rate that 'something is up'. The timing of the *coup* will therefore be dictated by the progress of our infiltration of the armed forces and police, and as soon as a satisfactory degree of penetration is achieved the *coup* must be executed. This implies that it will not be possible to designate a date well in advance of the *coup* which can be communicated to the various teams. This is just as well, since it means that the date cannot be leaked to the security agencies. Actually, it is quite likely that some information about us will have reached the security agencies, but this should not affect the outcome. As the preparations for the *coup* proceed, more and more information about our actions will be in circulation but it will also be increasingly obscured by 'noise'.*

Every move we make will generate information which could eventually reach the security agencies, but the consequences and misinterpretations of our actions will generate an equal or greater amount of 'noise'. This will make it increasingly difficult for the analysts of the security agencies to identify the nature of the threat, since their capacity for processing information is not unlimited. This process is illustrated by Figure 7, in which $O-Z$ is the normal level of 'noise' which is received at all times,

*An expression used in the Intelligence community to describe the false or irrelevant information which is reported alongside 'hard' data.

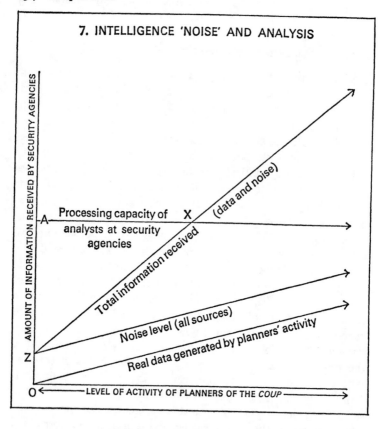

7. INTELLIGENCE 'NOISE' AND ANALYSIS

O–A is the processing capacity of the analysts at the security agencies, and *X* is the point beyond which the total flow of data exceeds processing capacity so that each item of real data is accorded a diminishing amount of attention.★

Even if the security agencies could isolate the real data from the 'noise', they will not usually take immediate action. Their professional instincts will be to try to explore all the ramifications of the plot so as to be able to arrest all its participants. And,

★The specialized nature of the security agencies' work impedes a rapid expansion of their facilities, and even if such an expansion could take place, it would only be carried out if and when the real threat is identified. This is precisely what the 'noise' problem prevents them from doing.

hopefully, the *coup* will actually take place while the security agencies are still engaged on these explorations. But the latter will be aware of this timing problem and are therefore likely to respond to a possible threat by going ahead and arresting those of the planners of the *coup* who have been identified. This 'nervousness' presents a special problem on the eve of the *coup* because our final preparations will probably generate a sharp increase in the total flow of information received by the security agencies. Even without separating hard data from 'noise', the mere increase in the total flow of information could be interpreted as a danger signal (as it certainly would be by competent analysts) and this might trigger off the arrests.

In practice, it will rarely be possible to achieve total security within the forces of the *coup* and we should assume as a working hypothesis that they have in fact been infiltrated by the security agency. This leads to the general defensive procedures discussed in Chapter 3, but it will also have precise operational implications:

(*a*) Each 'team' will be told well in advance what equipment and tactics will be required to seize its particular target, but not the exact designation of the target.

(*b*) Each 'team' will only be told its designated target when it actually receives the signal to proceed to its seizure.

(*c*) Each team will be alerted individually: with only as much advance warning as it requires to prepare for its particular task, instead of a general go-signal for all teams.

Since the teams will have different starting points and different targets to go to, the use of any one general signal would either give insufficient warning to some teams or an unnecessarily long one to others. The longer the time-span between the announcement that the *coup* is 'on' and its actual execution, the greater is the likelihood that information will reach the security agencies in time to prevent the successful execution of the *coup*, since this will be the moment at which their operative in our ranks could send out a warning.

The problem of warning-time and lead-time is illustrated in Figure 8.

If we give all our teams a ten-hour warning period, by sending

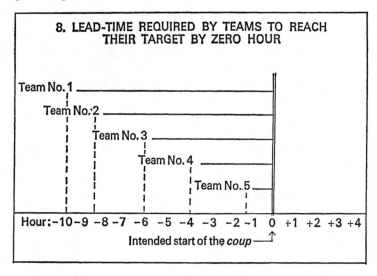

8. LEAD-TIME REQUIRED BY TEAMS TO REACH THEIR TARGET BY ZERO HOUR

Team No. 1 ─────────────────

Team No. 2 ───────────────

Team No. 3 ──────────

Team No. 4 ─────────

Team No. 5 ──

Hour: −10 −9 −8 −7 −6 −5 −4 −3 −2 −1 0 +1 +2 +3 +4

Intended start of the *coup* ─↑

out a general call at hour − 10, then team No. 1 will just about reach its target in time, but all the other teams will have received 'excess warning', or in other words, information will have been distributed before it was essential to do so. If we give all the teams a two-hour warning period, then 'excess warning' will be zero but team No. 5 will reach its target several hours before team No. 1 and those defending it will probably be on a full alert. The solution appears to be a simple one: make warning-time equal to lead-time so that each team is alerted just in time to allow it to reach its target by the zero hour.

But in reality the problem is more complex. It is not a matter of simultaneous arrival at the target but rather of the simul-taneous penetration of the 'early warning system' maintained by the security agencies of the state. If, for example, team No. 2 has to cross the entire capital city to reach its target, the security agency will probably be alerted as soon as it enters the city at, say, hour − 2. Thus by the time that team No. 4 reached its target, the opposition would have had two hours to prepare for its defence. We will probably have very little information on the functioning of the security apparatus, but we can operate on the assumption that a team (if it is large and/or equipped with armour) will be noticed and reported as soon as it enters the capital city. We must therefore secure: (*a*) the protection of our security position against an internal threat, which is achieved by minimizing 'excess warning time', and (*b*) the protection of our security position against external observation, which is achieved by simultaneous penetration of the capital city area.

Both aims will be achieved by sending the teams into action at a time corresponding to their 'lead-times' to the capital city boundary (or other applicable perimeter). This is illustrated in Figure 9.*

Into Action

The actual execution of the *coup* will require many different qualities: skilful diplomacy at a blocking position confronted by loyalist forces; instant personnel management at the radio-television station in order to persuade its technical staff to co-operate with us; considerable tactical abilities in the case of targets which are heavily defended. Our resources will probably be too limited to form fully-specialized teams out of the pool of those units and individuals which we have incorporated, but we should nevertheless match broad categories of targets with appropriate teams. We can distinguish between three such categories of targets and their corresponding teams:

A-TARGETS

These are the more heavily guarded facilities with strict pass control, such as the Royal or Presidential palace, the central police station and the army HQ. In times of crisis, of course, such facilities may be provided with fully-fledged military defences, and in many countries the crisis is permanent. Partly in order to minimize bloodshed, which could have a destabilizing effect on the situation and partly in order to reduce the total

*In the diagram the 'early warning system' is shown as a clearly delineated perimeter but, of course, in reality it will be a general area with vaguely defined borders. We will adopt as a perimeter whichever approximation suits the circumstances.

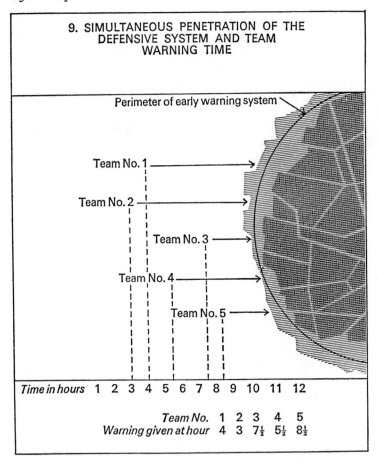

9. SIMULTANEOUS PENETRATION OF THE DEFENSIVE SYSTEM AND TEAM WARNING TIME

Team No.	1	2	3	4	5
Warning given at hour	4	3	7½	5½	8½

manpower required, these targets will have to be seized by 'sophisticated' teams using a blend of infiltration, diversion and assault.*

Though it will usually be necessary to prepare for a fairly extensive military operation (and a complex one as well, unless we have great numerical superiority in the area of the target) this should not result in much actual combat: when those who guard the target in question are confronted by our extensive

*The operational detail involved is discussed in Appendix B.

preparations, they are unlikely to put up much serious resistance. The fact that our general measures of neutralization have cut off or impeded their contacts with the leadership, the fact that the clear patriotic issues of international warfare will be missing in an internal conflict, and the fact that we will make every effort to allow them to give in gracefully, will all militate against a prolonged defence.

If we are fortunate enough to have incorporated a very large number of troops, and especially if they are equipped with impressive weapons, such as armour, it will be still less likely that actual combat will take place. These targets will nevertheless indirectly present us with a very serious problem, though it is political rather than military: the formation of the large teams required by these targets will raise the delicate issue of the *coup*-within-the-*coup*. During the active phase of the *coup* the situation will be confused and extremely unstable and while the other teams will be too small to tempt their leaders into trying to usurp our control, the operational leaders of the A-teams may well succumb to temptation. The man who leads the tanks which have just seized the Presidential Palace may easily persuade himself that he can also seize power on his own behalf and if the A-team is sufficiently powerful, he may do just that. Our satisfaction at having carried out a *coup* successfully would be an insufficient reward for all our efforts unless we also retain power afterwards. It will therefore be necessary to adopt measures to prevent the leaders of these large teams from challenging our position: this can sometimes be done by forming the A-teams from many small sub-units under the overall command of an inner member of our own group. Where this is not possible, the A-teams will have to be dispersed into smaller groups assigned to secondary targets as soon as they have fulfilled their primary mission. Thus the possible threat presented by the A-teams will be deflected by applying the energies of their leaders to other tasks. The operational commanders of the A-teams will probably need a certain amount of time to readjust to the fact that they are no longer isolated individuals engaged on a dangerous endeavour and to start thinking in more ambitious terms. Matters should be so arranged that they are deprived of their large and unified teams before the transition is made in their minds.

B-TARGETS

These are the technical facilities which will not usually be heavily guarded, and which in any case we want to neutralize rather than seize, such as the telephone exchange, the telegraph office and secondary radio-television stations. Each of those targets will be assigned to a small team whose personnel will include a 'technician' whose presence should help to minimize the amount of physical damage resulting from sabotage. If it is possible to interdict these targets by minor and external sabotage, the B-team may consist of just one or two technically-competent operators. Even if the actual building has to be entered for a short time, the B-team will still be a small one, but in this case it should be overt and consist of uniformed soldiers or policemen.

C-TARGETS

These are the individuals we wish to hold in isolation for the duration of the *coup*. In the case of the main leader(s) of the government, the arrests will be subsumed in the seizure of the Presidential Palace and similar A-targets, and therefore the other C-targets should not present a penetration problem. But they will present an evasion problem. A radio station or a Royal palace can be very difficult targets to seize but at least they cannot escape or conceal their identity. The personalities whom we wish to arrest will try to do both. It will therefore be essential to devote our early attentions to these targets so as to ensure that they are seized before they can evade our teams. This will usually imply that the C-teams will go into operation marginally earlier than the other teams, and they can do so without breaking the rule of simultaneous penetration of the 'early warning system', because they should be sufficiently small and dispersed to act covertly.

Because those targets are human they will be inherently more problematic than some of our other objectives; the individuals concerned, apart from escaping or concealing their identity, could also try to subvert the very teams sent to arrest them. In the case of particularly charismatic figures, our teams will have to be formed from especially selected personnel; in some cases it may even be necessary to include an inner member of our group. These C-teams will be small, since their task will be a matter of entering a private residence and overpowering one or two guards. The exact size of each team will depend on the over-all balance of resources and requirements under which we operate, but will rarely exceed a dozen men or so.

Once the individuals which form this group of targets have been arrested, we will have to ensure that they are kept under a secure form of control. Our purpose in arresting them is to prevent them from using their influence and/or charisma against us and this can only be achieved if we can insulate them from their public for the whole duration of the *coup*. Such individuals are often the only casualties of otherwise bloodless *coups*, because it is often easier to eliminate them, rather than to keep them as captives; if we do keep them, the *ad hoc* prison used must be both secret and internally secure. The liberation of a popular public figure could be a powerful focus of counter-*coup* actions on the part of the opposition and secrecy will be a more reliable defence than any physical barrier.

While the teams are on their way to their respective targets our other allies will also come into action: the individuals we have subverted in various parts of the armed forces and bureau-cracy will carry out their limited missions of technical neutraliza-tion. And the groups assigned to the blocking positions will be moving to take up their planned locations designed to isolate the loyalist forces. In the case of these dispersed individuals, whose contribution will be extremely important though almost totally invisible, there will be a signalling problem: since they are scattered throughout the sensitive parts of the state apparatus, it will be difficult to reach them individually. Further, they may include informants of the security agencies because, unlike the personnel of the various teams and blocking forces, they have been recruited as isolated individuals and therefore the mutual surveillance exercised on our behalf in the teams will not operate. Thus it would be dangerous to give them advance warning of the *coup* and their signal to go into action will have to be our first broadcast on the radio-television station, except in particular cases where the facility to be neutralized requires early attention.

Our operational control over the various groups cooperating with us will aim at achieving two objectives: (*a*) as always, maximum speed in the execution of their tasks, and (*b*) the use of the absolute minimum of force. This will be important not only because of the psychological and political factors previously mentioned, but also for a more direct, technical reason: the external uniformity between the two sides of the conflict. Our teams will, of course, be nationals of the country in which the *coup* is being staged, and most of them will be soldiers and police-men wearing the same uniforms as those of the opposition. This uniformity will give us a measure of protection since the loyalist forces will not readily know who is loyal and who is not. Usually it would be a mistake to prejudice this protective cover by adopting distinctive armbands or other conventional labels, since we will need all the protection we can get. Thus, as the teams move around the capital city (probably at night) they will probably not be fired upon, unless they open fire first; to do so would be to facilitate the work of the opposition since this will be their only way of distinguishing between their own forces and ourselves. Further, since our teams have always been kept separate, initially to prevent the penetration of the security agencies, and now to protect our own position within the forces of the *coup*, there will be a danger of conflict between our own teams. The confusion we generate in the minds of the opposition could therefore exact a price in confusion within our own ranks; this may have serious consequences unless our forces respect the rule of a minimal and purely defensive use of force.

The Immediate Post-Coup Situation

Once our targets have been seized, the loyalist forces isolated and the rest of the bureaucracy and armed forces neutralized, the active (and more mechanical) phase of the *coup* will be over.

But everything will still be in the balance: the old regime will have been deprived of its control over the critical parts of the mechanism of the state, but we ourselves will not yet be in control of it, except in a purely physical sense and then only in the area of the capital city. If we can retain our control over what we have seized, those political forces whose primary requirement is the preservation of law and order will probably give us their allegiance. Our objective, therefore, is to freeze the situation so that this process can take place. Thus, while until the actual execution of the *coup* our aim was to destabilize the situation, afterwards all our efforts should be directed at stabilizing or rather re-stabilizing, it.

We will be doing this at three different levels: (*a*) among our own forces, where our aim is to prevent our military or police allies from usurping our leadership; (*b*) within the state bureaucracy, whose allegiance and cooperation we wish to secure; and (*c*) with the public at large, whose acceptance we want to gain. In each case we will be using our leverage within one level in order to control the next one, but each level will also require separate and particular measures.

STABILIZING OUR OWN FORCES

During the planning stage, our recruits in the armed forces will be fully conscious of the fact that the success of the *coup* – and their own safety – depends on the work of coordination which we perform. Immediately after the *coup*, however, the only manifestation of all our efforts will be the direct force which they themselves control. In these circumstances they may well be tempted into trying a *coup* of their own, and they could do this by establishing contact with the other military leaders we have recruited, so as to secure their agreement to our exclusion from the leadership. Apart from the dispersal counter-measures discussed above, our only effective defence will be to retain full control over all 'horizontal' communications, or in other words to remain the only contact between each military leader we have recruited and his colleagues. This can sometimes be done technically by keeping under our control the actual communication equipment linking the various units, but this would only be effective in unusually extensive capital cities and would, in any case, break down after a relatively short period of time. Usually, we will need somewhat less direct political and psychological methods designed to keep apart the various military leaders we have recruited. This may involve promises of accelerated promotion to selected younger officers who could not otherwise expect very rapid advancement even within the limited context of those who have participated in the *coup*; it will also be useful to remind our military and police allies that their colleagues outside the conspiracy may try to displace them *en bloc* unless they – and we – form a tight and mutually supporting group. In general, we should ensure that all those who could pose an internal threat are kept occupied on tasks which, whether essential or not, will at least absorb their energies, and that there are divisive factors operating between them. As soon as we begin to receive the allegiance of military and bureaucratic leaders who were previously outside the conspiracy our leverage with our military and police recruits will increase very substantially. The problem of retaining control against such internal threats will therefore be largely short-term. As soon as our position has been established our best policy may be to dispose of our dangerous allies by using the usual polite methods available for the purpose: diplomatic posting abroad, nominal and/or remote command positions and 'promotions' to less vital parts of the state apparatus. Since it is possible that an embryonic *coup* has existed within our forces from the very beginning, the general security measures we designed to protect ourselves against the penetration of the security agencies will also serve a useful supplementary function: they will prevent the lateral spread of the conspiracy. If our internal security procedures are sufficiently good to prevent all contact between the separate 'cells', so that any infiltration by the security agencies is contained, they will also prevent the co-ordination of this inner opposition.

It has been calculated* that in a defensive military situation

---

*The calculations are based on the performance of ex-Soviet Ukrainian and Usbek troops used by the Germans in defensive positions during the Normandy landings in the Second World War.

even if only twenty per cent of the troops of a unit are loyal, the units concerned should operate successfully and perform their assigned function. And though in aggregate terms our forces will be operating offensively, *vis-à-vis* the uninfiltrated forces of the state, their outlook will be defensive both psychologically and tactically. Thus, even though it would be unusual to have the complete loyalty of those who (since they joined our *coup* in the first place) must be to some extent inherently disloyal, our forces should still perform successfully.

STABILIZING THE BUREAUCRACY

Our attitude towards the second level, the armed forces and bureaucracy which were not infiltrated before the *coup*, will depend partly on the degree of control which we have over our own 'incorporated' forces. Assuming that we have a reasonably firm hold over them, we should not try to extract any early commitment from the majority of soldiers and bureaucrats whose first information of our existence will be the *coup* itself. Not knowing the extent of the conspiracy, their principal pre-occupation will be the possible danger to their positions in the hierarchy: if most of the officers of the armed forces or the officials of a ministry have joined the *coup*, those who have not are hardly likely to be rewarded subsequently by rapid promotion. If the soldiers and bureaucrats realized that the group participating in the *coup* was in reality quite small, they would also realize the strength of their own position: the fact that they are collectively indispensable to *any* government, including the one to be formed after the *coup*. In the period immediately after the *coup*, however, they will probably see themselves as isolated individuals whose careers, and even lives, could be in danger. This feeling of insecurity may precipitate two alternative reactions, both extreme: they will either step forward to assert their loyalty to the leaders of the *coup* or else they will try to foment or join in opposition against us. Both reactions are undesirable from our point of view. Assertions of loyalty will usually be worthless since they are made by men who have just abandoned their previous, and possibly more legitimate, masters; opposition will always be dangerous and sometimes disastrous. Our policy towards the military and bureaucratic cadres will be to reduce this sense of insecurity; we should establish direct communication with as many of the more senior officers and officials as possible to convey one principal idea in a forceful and convincing manner: that the *coup* will not threaten their positions in the hierarchy and the aims of the *coup* do not include a reshaping of the existing military or administrative structures.* This requirement will incidentally have technical implications in the planning stage, when the sabotage of the means of communication must be carried out so as to be easily reversible.

The information campaign over the mass media will also reach this narrow but important section of the population, but it would be highly desirable to have more direct and confidential means of communication with them. The general political aims of the *coup* as expressed in our pronouncements on the radio and television will help to package our tacit deal with the bureaucrats and soldiers, but its real content will be the assurance that their careers are not threatened. In dealing with particular army or police officers who control especially important forces or with important bureaucrats, we may well decide to go further, in the sense that an actual exchange of promises of mutual support may take place. We should, however, remember that our main strength lies in the fact that only we have a precise idea of the extent of our power. It would therefore be unwise to enter into agreements which indicate that we need support urgently; more generally, any information which reveals the limits of our capabilities could threaten our position, which is essentially based on the fact that our inherent weakness is concealed. Again, as in the case of our own incorporated forces, we should make every effort to prevent communication between the cadres of the armed forces and bureaucracy outside our group. Such communication would usually be indispensable to those

---

*Even when the *coup* is a vehicle for a political group which seeks to achieve fundamental social change, the short-term objective is to stabilize the bureaucracy and the armed forces. Later, when alternative sources of direct force and political support have been established, the machinery of state can be re-shaped into an instrument suitable for revolutionary change.

who may seek to stage a counter-*coup*; the ignorance of the extent of the conspiracy will discourage such consultations: it is obviously dangerous to ask somebody to participate in the opposition to a group of which he is himself a member. But we should also interfere with such consultations directly, by using our control of the transport and communications infrastructure.

FROM POWER TO AUTHORITY: STABILIZING THE MASSES

The masses have neither the weapons of the military nor the administrative facilities of the bureaucracy, but their attitude to the new government established after the *coup* will ultimately be decisive. Our immediate aim will be to enforce public order, but our long-term objective is to gain the acceptance of the masses so that physical coercion will no longer be needed in order to secure compliance with our orders. In both phases we shall use our control over the infrastructure and the means of coercion, but as the *coup* recedes in time, political means will become increasingly important, physical ones less so.

Our first measures, to be taken immediately after the active phase of the *coup*, will be designed to freeze the situation by imposing physical immobility. A total curfew, the interruption of all forms of public transport, the closing of all public buildings and facilities and the interruption of the telecommunication services, will prevent, or at any rate impede active resistance to us. Organized resistance will be very difficult since there will be no way of inspiring and coordinating our potential opponents; unorganized resistance on the part of a mob will, on the other hand, be prevented because the people who might form such a mob would have to violate the curfew while acting as individuals, and not many will do this without the protective shelter of anonymity which a crowd provides.

The impact of our physical measures will be reduced outside the capital city but, to the extent that the capital city is the focus of the national network of transport and communications, both physical movement and the flow of information will be impeded. The physical controls will be purely negative and defensive in character and our reliance on them could be minimal because their concomitant effect is to enhance the importance of the armed forces we have subverted.

Our second and far more flexible instrument will be our control over the means of mass communications; their importance will be particularly great because the flow of all other information will be affected by our physical controls. Moreover, the confused and dramatic events of the *coup* will mean that the radio and television services will have a particularly attentive and receptive audience. In broadcasting over the radio and television services our purpose is not to provide information about the situation but rather to affect its development by exploiting our monopoly of these media. We will have two principal objectives in the information campaign that will start immediately after the *coup*: (*a*) to discourage resistance to us by emphasizing the strength of our position, and (*b*) to dampen the fears which would otherwise give rise to such resistance.

Our first objective will be achieved by conveying the reality and strength of the *coup* instead of trying to justify it; this will be done by listing the controls we have imposed, by emphasizing that law and order have been fully restored, and by stating that all resistance has ceased. One of the major obstacles to active resistance will be the fact that we have fragmented the opposition so that each individual opponent would have to operate in isolation, cut off from friends and associates. In these circumstances the news of any resistance against us would act as a powerful stimulant to further resistance by breaking down this feeling of isolation. We must therefore make every effort to withhold such news. If there is in fact some resistance and if its intensity and locale are such as to make it difficult to conceal from particular segments of the public, we should admit its existence; but we should strongly emphasize that it is *isolated*, the product of the obstinacy of a few misguided or dishonest individuals who are not affiliated to any party or group of significant membership. The constant working of the *motif* of isolation, the repetition of long and detailed lists of the administrative and physical controls we have imposed and the emphasis on the fact that law and

TABLE 15. *The First Communiqué: A Choice of Styles*

The Romantic/Lyrical

'This is not a communiqué, but an avowal, an undertaking and an appeal. It is an avowal of the situation in which the Army and the People have been reduced by a handful of evil men ... it is an undertaking to wash clean the shame and disgrace suffered by the Army ... it is finally a call to arms and to honour. ...'

Captain Mustafa Hamdun, Aleppo Radio, 6.30 a.m.
   25 February 1954

The Messianic

'The bourgeoisie is abolished ... a new era of equality between all citizens is inaugurated ... all agreements with foreign countries will be respected. ...'

Colonel Jean Bedel Bokassa, Central African Republic,
   15 January 1966

The Unprepared

'... [This rebellion has been made for] a strong united and prosperous Nigeria free from corruption and internal strife. ... Looting, arson, *homosexuality* [*sic*], rape, embezzlement, bribery, corruption, sabotage and false alarm will be punishable by death. ...'

Major Nzeogwu, Radio Kaduna, Nigeria, 15 January 1966

The Rational-Administrative

'The myth surrounding Kwame N'krumah has been broken ... [he] ruled the country as if it were his private property ... [his] capricious handling of the country's economic affairs ... brought the country to the point of economic collapse. ... We hope to announce measures for curing the country's troubles within a few days ... the future definitely bright. ...'

Radio communiqué of Ghana's National Liberation Council
   February 1966

---

order have been re-established, should have the effect of making resistance appear as dangerous and useless.

The second objective of our information campaign will be to reassure the general public by dispelling fears that the *coup* is inspired by foreign and/or extremist elements, and to persuade particular groups that the *coup* is not a threat to them. The first aim will be achieved by manipulating national symbols and by asserting our belief in the prevailing pieties: in the Arab world the new regime will announce its belief in Arab unity and Islam, or Arab unity and socialism as the case may be; where, as in Egypt, the revolution has been institutionalized, it will be necessary to assert our belief in *Al-Thawra*. In Africa, the new regime will announce its intention of fighting tribalism at home and racialism abroad; in Latin America the need to secure social justice (or to fight Communism and perhaps *fidelismo*) will be invoked. Everywhere in the 'Third World', nationalist rhetoric will be used and references made to the glorious people of X and the glorious land of X which the last regime has degraded; above all, repeated denunciations of neo-, and not so neo-colonialism are *de rigueur*. Such denunciations will be particularly important where there is a large foreign business enterprise operating in the country in question; the inevitable suspicions that the *coup* is a product of the machinations of the 'Company' can only be dispelled by making violent attacks on it. These, being verbal and not unexpected, will pacify the public without disturbing the business interests, and the attacks should be all the more violent if these suspicions are in fact justified.

While the religious attitude leads to the praise of the gods for one's successes and self-blame for one's failures, the nationalist attitude is to attribute successes to the nation and to blame foreigners for its failures. Similarly, the chants in praise of the gods have been replaced by ritualized curses variously addressed to different groups of foreigners and their activities. Thus for the phrase 'the imperialist-neo-colonialist power *bloc*' read the English and the French if it is spoken by Africans of former colonies of those countries; while the phrase 'Zionist oil monopolist plotters' translates into Jews and Christians in the subconscious of the Muslim Arabs who make use of it.

There may be a purely ideological element in these denunciations, but even when the American extreme right speaks of 'the international conspiracy of godless Communism' it is significant that they stigmatize it as 'un-American' rather than as anticapitalist. We shall make use of a suitable selection of these un-lovely phrases; though their meaning has been totally obscured by constant and deliberate misuse,* they will be useful as indi-cators of our impeccable nationalism, and if that is not in reality our position they will serve to obscure our true policy aims.

The flow of information emanating from all the sources under our control should be coordinated with our other measures: the impositions of physical controls will be announced and explained, and the political moves, to which we now turn, will be suitably presented. Physical coercion will deter or defeat direct opposi-tion, while the information campaign will lay the basis of our eventual acquisition of authority, but only political means will secure for us a base of active support. Where the pre-*coup* regime was exceptionally brutal, corrupt or retrograde, the leaders of the *coup* will have little trouble in gaining a generalized form of acceptance but, even then, the active support of specific groups can only be gained by political accommodation, i.e. by sponsor-ing policies which serve the interests of particular groups thus giving them reasons for becoming committed to (or at least interested in) our survival. In some Latin American countries, for example, we could gain the support of the landless peasants by announcing our intention of carrying out a programme of agrarian reform. In West Africa we could announce our inten-tion of increasing the prices paid to peasant producers by the various commodity marketing boards; in Greece and Turkey, where there is a heavy burden of peasant indebtedness, we could announce a general cancellation of agrarian debts. Each of these policy announcements will bind the interests of a large and politically powerful group to our government unless we are overtaken by other rival announcements, but it will also lead to the hostility of other groups, whose interests are damaged by our intended policies. In Latin America, where the peasants would benefit, the landlords would lose; in Africa the urban population would be the loser while in Greece the taxpayer would bear the burden of peasant debt relief. Thus, the backing of one

*On 12 June 1967 the *East German* radio referred to the 'Nazi atrocities committed by Jews against the Arabs of Gaza', who were described as 'victims of a Zionist-revanchist-imperialist plot'.

interest group will generally have as its concomitant the loss of support of – or even actual hostility from – other groups. Clearly, it will be necessary to estimate the *net* political support which a given policy announcement will generate. This will mean taking into account not only the political significance of each group but also the immediacy of its political power. In the context of a Latin American post-*coup* situation, for example, the goodwill of remote and dispersed peasants will not help us much against the immediate and powerful opposition of bureaucratic and military cadres who could for the most part be the children of the land-owning aristocracy. If, on the other hand, our short-term position is strong but we are threatened by a longer-term usurpation of power on the part of our military allies, our objective will be to create a counter-weight capable eventually of becoming a source of direct strength, such as a peasants' militia. Thus whether we opt for a 'left' policy of land reform and longer-term *campesino* support, or a 'right' policy of peasant repression and immediate land-owner support, will depend on the balance between the strength of our short- and our long-term positions.

The almost mechanical elements which are important in the special climate of the immediate post-*coup* period, will distort the normal balance between the political forces of the country concerned. If, therefore, our short-term position is not fragile, we should repress the agitation of those forces which have a disproportionate strength in the short term and concentrate instead on cultivating the support of those groups whose longer-term strength is the greater.

An element in our strategy after the *coup* is half-way between the information and the political campaign; the problem of 'legitimizing' the *coup*. Clearly the *coup* is by definition illegal, but whether this illegality matters, and whether it is possible to counteract its effects, will depend on the total political environment of the country in question. We have seen in Chapter 2 that in much of the 'Third World' the legitimacy or otherwise of the government will not greatly matter; the government is treated as part of nature, that is, something that one adjusts to rather than questions. Elsewhere, however, the general attitude of the masses could be more legalistic. One way of legitimizing the post-*coup* government has already been mentioned in the discussion of the selection of the personalities to be arrested – the retention of the nominal head of state (where such a constitutional role exists) as our own highly nominal head of state. In this way, the appearance of continuity will be maintained and with it the appearance of legitimacy. Where the head of state is not nominal, as in 'presidential' regimes, other tactics will have to be used: the announcement of forthcoming elections or a referendum (as a sort of *ex-post facto* legitimization) or, alternatively, the *coup* can be openly admitted as an extra-constitutional intervention, but one made against an un-constitutional regime. One illegality will then be represented as being the cause of the other, but we shall declare that whereas the illegality of the pre-*coup* regime was *voluntary* and *permanent*, ours is *necessary* and *temporary*.

Such techniques will be of limited value in conducting the political processes required to create a base of active support and to secure our authority, since everything will depend on the particular political environment in which we shall be operating; one particular problem, however, requires further exploration: recognition by foreign powers. This is almost always important, but for many countries of the 'Third World', whose *pays réel* lies outside their own borders, it will be a crucial problem. When much of the available disposable funds come from foreign loans, investment or grants, and when foreign cadres carry out vital administrative, technical and sometimes even military functions, the maintenance of good relations with the particular 'donor' country or countries concerned may well be a determining factor in our political survival after the *coup*. Premature recognition by a foreign power, i.e. recognition granted while the old regime still retains some degree of control, is becoming regarded as a form of aggression in international law. Beyond this, however, recognition is usually granted to illegitimate governments after a polite interval if there are convincing assurances about their continuity in terms of foreign relations. These assurances are conveyed simply and publicly by formal announcements stating that membership in alliances and groupings will be maintained, that foreign agreements and obligations will be respected and that legitimate foreign interests in the country concerned will not be harmed. Thus the leaders of Ghana's National Liberation Council, which was formed after N'krumah's overthrow, announced that Ghana would retain her membership of the Commonwealth, the Organization of African Unity and of the UN, and would respect all obligations undertaken by N'krumah's regime. Similarly, Arab post-*coup* regimes announce that they will remain in the Arab League, and Latin American regimes, in the Organization of American States. Far more important than these declarations is the considerable diplomacy activity which will take place after the *coup* (and sometimes even before it). The purpose of these diplomatic exchanges will be to clarify the political situation and, nowadays, to indicate – or to dissemble – the ideological orientation of the planners of the *coup*. Most countries of the world follow British diplomatic doctrine in granting recognition to regimes on the basis of the effective control of their territories. But this is a doctrine as flexible as the definition of 'control'; so that recognition can sometimes be withheld if the pre-*coup* regime retains control over some part of the national territory, as in the case of British non-recognition of the Yemeni Republican regime.

After the necessary exchanges of information and assurances, the new government will usually be recognized; this will be so even if its illegality is an embarrassment, as in the case of the United States and Latin American *coups*, or if its ideological orientation is distasteful, as in the case of the Soviet Union and the Ghanaian and Indonesian *coups*.

Diplomatic recognition is one of the elements in the general process of establishing the authority of the new government; until this is achieved, we will have to rely on the brittle instruments of physical coercion and our position will be vulnerable to many threats – including that of *coup d'état*.

Appendix A

The Economics of Repression

Once we have carried out our *coup* and established control over the bureaucracy and the armed forces, our long-term political survival will largely depend on our management of the problem of economic development. Economic development is generally regarded as a 'good thing' and almost everybody wants more of it, but for us – the newly-established government of X-land – the pursuit of economic development will be undesirable, since it militates against our main goal: political stability.

An economy develops by extending and improving its stock of human and physical capital and this requires investment, whether to train people or to build factories. In order to invest, current income has to be withdrawn from would-be consumers and channelled away to create capital. Clearly, the higher the rate of investment the faster will be the development of the economy, but also the lower the *present* standard of living. The governments of economically backward countries – where the need for development is manifest – are therefore faced with the alternative of either slow economic development or further reduction of the already desperately low standard of living. The more that can be taxed from current incomes, the nearer will be the beautiful dawn of prosperity – even if it is the prosperity of Spain or Greece rather than that of Western Europe or North America. But there are limits to the amount of saving that can be forced out of a population whose annual income per head is already very low: there is an economic survival limit below which the population – or a large part of it – would simply starve (or retreat into the pure subsistence economy), but well before this point is reached, there is a political survival limit below which *we*, as the government would be overthrown. The economic survival limit is more or less rigid: in any particular environment with a given climate, pattern of nutrition, habits and traditions, there will be a minimum annual income which an inhabitant of average resourcefulness will need to satisfy his and his family's bodily needs. The 'political survival limit' is, however, very flexible and it will depend on psychological, historical and social factors, but also on the efficiency of the system of state security and of the propaganda machine.

The problem is particularly acute in the newly-independent states of the 'Third World'. The colonial regimes may or may not have tried to achieve economic development, but if they did try it was without the urgency which the new post-colonial regimes try to achieve. Immediately after independence, there-fore, instead of the increase in the standard of living which the native population had been led to expect, the opposite takes place. The new 'independence' government has to increase taxes and import duties in order to finance the great projects with which economic development often starts: dams, road systems, steel mills and harbours. Foreign aid, which many in the 'donor' countries have been led to believe to be very substantial,* only contributes a fraction of the necessary funds. Most of the money has to come out of current incomes so that, instead of 'having cars like the whites', the level of consumption actually falls. This impoverishment of those who are already very poor indeed is not easily tolerated – especially when the mecha-nism of expectations has been built up.

Our basic problem, therefore, is to achieve economic develop-ment – in order to satisfy the aspirations of the *élite* and would-be *élite*† – without taxing the masses beyond the politically safe limit, which could lead to their revolt. There are two main instruments with which we can persuade the masses to accept the sacrifice of present consumption for the sake of an increased future income: propaganda and repression‡ or, more efficiently, by a mixture of both. Imagine, therefore, that we have inherited

---

*Foreign aid has been *falling* as a percentage of GNP in the developed countries in the last few years.

†For the *élite*, economic development subsumes the national goal of modernization with the personal goal of expanded career opportunities. For the new generation of educated citizens (the would-be *élite*) economic development is a guarantee of employment – and the unemployed intelli-gentsia is a major threat to many regimes in the 'Third World'.

‡By propaganda is meant the whole range of activities whose content is information or entertainment and whose function, in this case, is (*a*) to

a country with a backward economy whose vital statistics are
those shown in Table 16.

TABLE 16. *National Accounts Data, Country X. (Assumed*
egalitarian distribution)

Annual GNP per head		
£100	...	Present actual level of income in pounds per inhabitant
£90	...	Level of taxation accepted in the past (i.e. net income left after tax)
£80		
£70		
£60		
£50		
£45	...	Economic survival limit
£40		
£30		
£20		
£10		

Thus, in the past, in this poor (but not particularly poor)
country the gross national product per head was £100 per year,
and of this £10 was paid out in various taxes while £90 was
spent on current consumption, or saved. Now we know that only
£45 per inhabitant per year is needed for economic survival, and
the problem is to get hold of some of the difference in order to

distract attention from present hardship, (*b*) to justify it in terms of assured
future happiness. This may or may not involve the presentation of the
outside world as even less well off, but it will almost certainly present the
past standard of living as much inferior. An equally important aim of
propaganda will be to persuade the masses that the present leadership is
the most efficient vehicle for modernization; this can be done in rational
terms by using statistical images, or by irrational ones which present the
leadership as super-human. By repression is meant the whole range of
political police activities which aim at: (*a*) suppressing individual political
activity by surveillance and imprisonment, (*b*) intimidating the masses by
displays of force, and (*c*) preventing the circulation of rival information by
controlling the media and inhibiting public discussion.

finance development – and to do so without being overthrown. If we simply increase taxes the chances are that part of the population will refuse to pay them, and if administrative methods are used in order to enforce payment a violent reaction may ensue. We will therefore divert some of the modest tax payments received now (£10 in the diagram) from other uses, and spend it on propaganda and the police. This may well result in the situation shown in Table 17.

TABLE 17. *National Accounts Data, Country X. (After propaganda and police)*

Annual GNP per head		
£100	...	Present actual level of income per inhabitant
£90		
£80	...	Level of taxation accepted after, say, £1 per head per year has been spent on propaganda and police
£70		
£60		
£50		
£45	...	Economic survival limit
£40		
£30		
£20		
£10		

In the new situation, then, our sums work out as in Table 18.

TABLE 18. *National Accounts Data, Country X. (Funds available for development)*

Before	(Expenditure on propaganda and repression)	After
£100	←———— GNP per head per year ————→	£100
£55	←— Less £45 per year needed for 'survival' —→	£55
£10	←——————Tax collected ———————→	£20
£0	←Less money spent on propaganda and repression →	£1
£10	←——— Net funds available for development ———→	£19

Thus by spending £1 per man per year on propaganda and an efficient police system, we have lowered the political survival limit by £10, and after deducting the amount spent on the system of repression and persuasion we still have £19 left. If we spend another £1 per man per year the chances are that we will be able to 'liberate' some more of the possible margin above the survival limit, but as we spend more and more money on repression we are likely to find that it will lower the safety limit by less and less (see Figure 10). And, of course, as we spend more and more on the police and propaganda we will find that while the first extra £10 of taxes costs us £1 to obtain with safety, the next £10 will cost, say, £2. Eventually the point is reached where (as shown in Figure 10) further expenditure brings us no increase in taxation at all. At that point we spend an extra

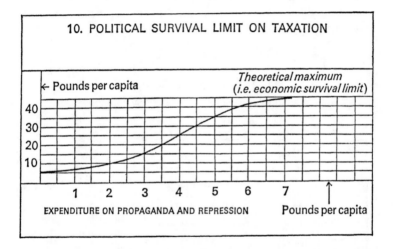

£1 per year and get no increase at all in the taxes which can safely be collected. Well before that point is reached, however, there will be an earlier stage when we will spend, say, an extra £1 on repression and persuasion and get exactly the same sum in further taxes. Immediately before *that* point is the *maximum efficiency* level of expenditure on the police and propaganda machine.

Maximum Safety and Zero Economic Development

This is the formula which Duvalier has applied in Haiti with increasing thoroughness since his rise to power. Taxation, which is heavy for a country with an annual income per head of about £30, is spent almost entirely on the army, the 'police' (the Ton Ton Macoutes) and on propaganda. The only major economic development project is of doubtful value: the building of a new capital, 'Duvalierville', which, in any case, has now been suspended.

The Duvalier mix of efficient repression, massive propaganda and no development investment has paid off; he has been in power continuously since September 1957, and his regime still appears to be more stable than that of most Latin American countries. The Ton Ton Macoutes operate as a semi-public presidential guard which carries out police and security functions, and they supplement their (generous) salaries by private exac-

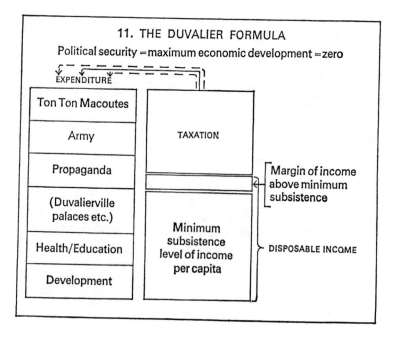

11. THE DUVALIER FORMULA

Political security = maximum economic development = zero

tions from what is left of the business sector. The propaganda machine, which involves ceremonial parades, laudatory films and the projection of 'Papa Doc' as a Voodoo expert, is almost as expensive to run as the Ton Ton Macoutes, but equally useful. The extreme poverty of the population means that their level of political awareness and even vitality is extremely low; the Ton Ton Macoutes terrorize the thin *élite* and the army officers – who are constantly watched – and the Ton Ton themselves rely on Duvalier because their position depends on his survival; the Voodoo mythology and the propaganda machine have deified the man whom the Ton Ton defend, and if Duvalier should disappear from the scene the army and/or the masses would quickly liquidate the Ton Ton.

Kwame N'krumah of Ghana, and many other African leaders now dead, in prison or in exile, have followed a policy of high taxation and investment associated with clearly insufficient propaganda and repression effort. N'krumah in spite of his eccentricities, was largely defeated by his own success: the by-product of the considerable economic development achieved by Ghana was to stimulate and educate the masses and the new *élite*, their attitude to N'krumah's regime becoming more and more critical in the light of the education which the regime itself provided. When this happens, more and more repression and propaganda are needed to maintain political stability and, in spite of considerable efforts, N'krumah was unable to build a sufficiently ruthless police system. The cause of his downfall was not, therefore, the mismanagement of the economy – which was considerable – but rather the success of much of the development effort.

The middle way, efficient repression, extensive propaganda and enough economic development to create new *élites* committed to the regime, has been followed successfully in both the Soviet Union and China; the regimes of both countries have, however, used different blends of repression and propaganda. The two are interchangeable up to a point, but the nature of the most efficient mixture will depend on the particular country, and local conditions will dictate the most appropriate mixture.

Appendix B

Tactical Aspects of the *Coup d'Etat*

In the decisive (active) phase of the *coup* the forces which we have acquired by infiltrating and subverting the system of state security will be used to seize certain objectives or to neutralize selected facilities. To do this force will be essential, but since bloodshed could have unfortunate destabilizing effects we should arrange matters so that the threat of force will suffice to achieve our objectives, rather than its actual use. In this appendix we will analyse two main problems, (*a*) the formation of the active teams and their operational use, and (*b*) the deployment of the blocking forces. In both cases our two major preoccupations will be to avoid or minimize bloodshed and – more important – to ensure that our position is not threatened after the *coup* by a usurpation of our power on the part of the soldiers and policemen we have recruited.

The Formation of the Active Teams

Our infiltration of the armed forces and police of the state may have been either general and diffuse or concentrated within a few large formations. In the first type of infiltration the forces we have subverted will consist of many small sub-units, whose commanders have decided to join us while their more senior colleagues – who command the unit as a whole – have remained outside the scope of our infiltration; in the second type of infiltration a few large units have come over to us *en bloc* with all, or most, of their entire establishment. The two alternatives are illustrated in Table 19.

Both types of infiltration have their advantages and disadvantages: if we have subverted many small sub-units we will have some additional protective cover, since the supporters of the pre-*coup* regime will not readily be able to identify which units have remained loyal and which have joined us; it will also be useful to be able to confront loyalist forces with teams made

TABLE 19. *Eve of the coup: forces of the state fully subverted (notional)*

Diffuse — infiltration —	*Concentrated*
3 companies of brigade X	2 battalions of brigade X
6 companies of brigade Y	1 battalion of brigade Y
7 companies of brigade Z	
1 battalion of brigade V	
4 companies of brigade U	
Total forces = 3,000 men	Total forces = 3,000 men

up from their own cadres. The subversion of a few large units, on the other hand, will minimize the problems of coordination and recognition and, more important, will increase the security level before the *coup*, since within each large unit there would be a measure of mutual surveillance which would deter defections to the regime or leaks to the security agencies. After the active phase of the *coup*, however, a composite force made up of many small sub-units will be much more secure since it will reduce the risk of a usurpation of our position on the part of our military allies. This would be so for three main reasons: (*a*) the rank of the officers concerned will obviously be lower if they are the appointed commanders of small units rather than large ones, (*b*) it will be easier to disperse our forces after the active phase of the *coup* if their concentration is not organic but a construct of our own, and (*c*) the larger the number of independent unit leaders involved in the *coup* the less likely they are to combine in order to exclude us from power.

Whatever the sources of the forces which we have incorporated, it will often be necessary to restructure them for the purposes of the *coup*, since the many specialized tasks to be carried out will require widely different teams; only if we have numerical superiority or its equivalent over the loyalist forces will we be able to use the formations we have subverted in their natural state. We will need three types of team, as well as the blocking forces, and these will correspond to the three types of targets discussed in Chapter 5, and we will therefore draw on the pool of subverted units and individuals to form the required number of A-, B- and C-teams.

The A-teams will be needed in order to seize the major defended objectives, such as the residence of the ruler, the main radio-television station and the army and police headquarters. These will be both larger in size and more sophisticated in structure than the other two types of team. Each A-team will consist of four elements whose relative size will vary with each particular target:

(a) a 'civilian' penetration group. This will be very small and will consist of a few men in civilian clothes carrying concealed weapons or explosives. Their function will be to enter the target as open and legitimate 'visitors' in order to assist in its seizure from the inside. This assistance can be a direct internal assault, or it can take the form of an internal diversion; in the case of the broadcasting facility, however, their main function will be to prevent the use of its installations to raise the alarm.

(b) a 'diversion' group. This group will be important in proportion to the size of the forces deployed to protect the target. Where, as in the case of the royal or presidential palace, there could be an entire infantry formation assigned to protect the target, a diversion, designed to attract part of the loyalist forces, will be essential. The diversion group will carry out its function by creating a disturbance, or by actually carrying out an assault on a near-by secondary target. The diversion should be timed to include the reaction time of the loyalist forces and their route time to the scene of the disturbance, after which the main assault on the primary target will take place.

(c) a covering 'fire' group. This will be a small group but it will include troops with heavier weapons, especially armoured fighting vehicles. Its function will be to deter resistance on the part of the loyalists, by giving demonstrations of fire-power, and to prevent the intervention of loyalist forces from elsewhere by covering approach routes.

(d) an assault group. This will be by far the largest, and its

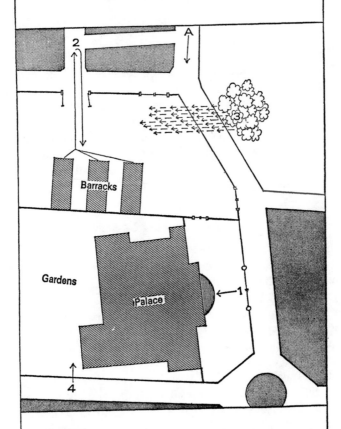

12. 'SOPHISTICATED' SEIZURE OF MAJOR DEFENDED TARGETS

SEQUENCE

1. Civilian penetration

2. Diversion designed to attract loyalist troops away from palace

3. Interdicting fire to prevent their return and the passage of the main loyalist forces

4. Assault group from street enters into action

A. Expected approach of main loyalist forces

members should be chosen on the usual criteria of combat proficiency, though hopefully their skills will not be needed.

The integrated operation of the different groups of each A-team is illustrated in Figure 12.

The B- and C-teams, whose function is respectively to arrest political personalities and to sabotage selected facilities, will not face significant tactical problems and their organization will be a matter of forming small teams equipped with suitable transport, of designating the target and of coordinating the timing. Each team will consist of a couple of jeep-loads of troops or police accompanied by a member of our inner group – in the case of the major political personalities – or by a technician – in the case where the sabotage requires a measure of expertise.

The Deployment of the Blocking Forces

Although it is to be hoped that the pre-*coup* regime will be unaware of the timing of our particular *coup*, it will probably be conscious of the danger from *coups* in general. Regimes in politically unstable countries often go to great lengths to maintain a force of politically reliable troops or armed police on which they can rely against threats to internal security. Its officers and men often share the ethnic and/or religious affiliation of the ruling group and special safeguards are employed to ensure its political reliability. The infiltration of such 'palace guards' is very difficult, and we may well have deliberately decided to exclude them from the scope of our infiltration. Elsewhere, even where every major force has been fully subverted or internally neutralized, we will still be vulnerable to unexpected defections or coincidental transfers of uninfiltrated troops. For all these reasons, therefore, the blocking forces designed to insulate the capital city from the intervention of loyalist forces will be essential since, as has been repeatedly emphasized, the intervention of determined loyalist forces – however small in size –could have effects disproportionate to their size.

The operation of a blocking force is the exact opposite of an ambush: while the objective of an ambush is to inflict maximum

13. GENERAL STRUCTURE OF BLOCKING POSITION

Observation line to detect and prevent infiltration

Expected path of loyalist forces

Limit of area of
constrained passage

'Symbolic'
road blocks

Main defence forces
protected but not
concealed

Anti-tank/
tank positions

To capital city and political-administrative centre

damage without controlling passage, the objective of the blocking force is to prevent passage while inflicting minimum
damage. The general structure of the blocking position is shown
in Figure 13 but two essentials are missing: (*a*) correct intelligence about the location and intentions of the loyalist forces, and

(b) the efficient use of natural barriers (such as bridges, tunnels, densely built-up areas, etc.) and of subsidiary roadblocks to channel any loyalist force into the blocking position.

The area of constrained passage on the diagram represents the group of roads or streets which an intervention force must use in order to enter the city from a particular direction; it is not generally meant to represent a single road or street, though in particular settings this may be the case.

The 'observation line' (or 'screen' in military terminology) attempts to infiltrate round the blocking position which dismounted loyalist troops may make. The 'symbolic' roadblocks deployed across the set of roads or streets concerned will dissuade the loyalist forces by appealing to 'orders' and comradeship; if dissuasion fails, they will try deterrence by pointing out the main defensive forces and the anti-tank positions (or the tanks if available). The operational leadership of the main defensive forces, the 'teeth' of the blocking position, will have to be chosen carefully to ensure a determined defence if force is in fact used by the loyalist troops; they must also be made aware of the damaging consequences which could ensue if the blocking position degenerates into an ambush.

APPENDIX C

Statistics

TABLE I *Economic Development and the* Coup d'État, *1945-78*
Revised and updated by George Schott, August 8, 1978

NOTE: All data for the individual countries are from the *World Bank Atlas: Population, Per Capita Product, and Growth Rates,* World Bank, 1977. Data refer to 1976 except for 12 of the smaller countries for which the data refer to 1975.

Country	Per Capita Gross National Product Figures Dollars	Coup d'État?	Date of Last Successful coup
AFRICA			
Algeria	990	yes	1965
Angola	330	yes	–
Benin	130	yes	1972
Botswana	410	no	–
Burundi	120	yes	1976
Cameroon	290	no	–
Cape Verde	260	no	–
Central African Empire	230	yes	1966
Chad	120	yes	1975
Comoros	180	yes	1978
Djibouti	1,940	no	–
Egypt	280	yes	1952
Equatorial Guinea	330	yes	–
Ethiopia	100	yes	1974
Gabon	2,590	yes	–
Gambia	180	no	–
Ghana	580	yes	1972
Guinea	150	yes	–
Guinea-Bissau	140	no	–

Country	Per Capita Gross National Product Figures Dollars	Coup d'État?	Date of Last Successful coup
Ivory Coast	610	no	–
Kenya	240	no	–
Lesotho	170	yes	1970
Liberia	450	yes	–
Libya	6,310	yes	1969
Madagascar	200	yes	1975
Malawi	140	no	–
Mali	100	yes	1968
Mauritania	340	yes	1978
Mauritius	680	no	–
Morocco	540	yes	–
Mozambique	170	yes	–
Namibia	980	no	–
Niger	160	yes	1974
Nigeria	380	yes	1975
Réunion	1,920	no	–
Rhodesia	550	no	–
Rwanda	110	yes	1973
Senegal	390	no	–
Seychelles	580	yes	1977
Sao Tome and Principe	490	no	–
Sierra Leone	200	yes	1968
Somalia	110	yes	1969
South Africa	1,340	no	–
Sudan	290	yes	1969
Swaziland	470	yes	1973
Tanzania	180	yes	1964
Togo	260	yes	1967
Tunisia	840	no	–
Uganda	240	yes	1971

Country	Per Capita Gross National Product Figures Dollars	Coup d'État?	Date of Last Successful coup
Upper Volta	110	yes	1966
Zaire	140	yes	1965
Zambia	440	no	–
ASIA			
Afghanistan	160	yes	1978
Bangladesh	110	yes	1975
Bhutan	70	no	–
Burma	120	yes	1962
Cambodia	–*	yes	1970
China, People's Rep. of	410	no	–
Hong Kong	2,110	no	–
India	150	no	–
Indonesia	240	yes	–
Iran	1,930	no	–
Japan	4,910	no	–
Korea, Dem. People's Rep.	470	no	–
Korea, Rep. of	670	yes	1961
Laos	90	yes	1964
Macao	780	no	–
Maldives	110	no	–
Mongolia	860	no	–
Malaysia	860	no	–
Nepal	120	yes	1960
Pakistan	170	yes	1977

* In Kampuchean conditions no GNP estimate could have meaning.

Country	Per Capita Gross National Product Figures Dollars	Coup d'État?	Date of Last Successful coup
Philippines	410	no	–
Singapore	2,700	no	–
Sri Lanka	200	yes	–
Taiwan	1,070	no	–
Thailand	380	yes	1977
Vietnam	–*	yes	1965

LATIN AMERICA

Argentina	1,550	yes	1976
Bahamas	3,310	no	–
Barbados	1,550	no	–
Bolivia	390	yes	1978
Brazil	1,140	yes	1964
Chile	1,050	yes	1973
Colombia	630	yes	1957
Costa Rica	1,040	yes	–
Cuba	860	yes	1952
Dominican Republic	780	yes	1965
Ecuador	640	yes	1976
El Salvador	490	yes	1961
Grenada	420	no	–
Guadeloupe	1,500	no	–
Guatemala	690	yes	1963
Guyana	540	no	–
Haiti	200	yes	1950
Honduras	390	yes	1975

* For Vietnam the per capita GNP is tentatively estimated at $151.

Country	Per Capita Gross National Product Figures Dollars	Coup d'État?	Date of Last Successful coup
Jamaica	1,070	no	–
Martinique	2,350	no	–
Mexico	1,090	no	–
Netherlands Antilles	1,680	no	–
Nicaragua	750	yes	1947
Panama	1,310	yes	1968
Paraguay	640	yes	1954
Peru	800	yes	1975
Puerto Rico	2,430	no	–
Surinam	1,370	no	–
Trinidad and Tobago	2,240	yes	–
Uruguay	1,390	no	–
Venezuela	2,570	yes	1952

MIDDLE EAST/SOUTHWEST ASIA

Country	Per Capita GNP	Coup d'État?	Date of Last coup
Bahrain	2,410	no	–
Cyprus	1,480	yes	1974
Iraq	1,390	yes	1968
Israel	3,920	no	–
Jordan	610	no	–
Kuwait	15,480	no	–
Lebanon	–*	yes	–
Oman	2,680	yes	1970
Qatar	11,400	yes	1972
Saudi Arabia	4,480	no	–
Syria	780	yes	1970
Turkey	990	yes	1971

* The 1977 GNP is tentatively estimated at $2.9 Billion.

Country	Per Capita Gross National Product Figures Dollars	Coup d'État?	Date of Last Successful coup
United Arab Emirates	13,990	yes	
Yemen	250	yes	1974
Yemen, Democratic	280	yes	1978

EUROPE, NORTH AMERICA AND OCEANIA

Czechoslovakia	3,840	yes	1948
Greece	2,590	yes	1973
Portugal	1,690	yes	1974

TABLE II *Basic List of* Coups *and Attempted* Coups, *1945-78*
Revised and updated by George Schott, August 8, 1978

Date	Main Party	Outcome
AFRICA		
Algeria		
June 19, 1965	elements from three services	successful
Dec. 13, 1967	army faction	failed
Angola		
May 27, 1977	army and political faction	failed
Benin (Dahomey)		
Oct. 28, 1963	army faction	successful
Dec. 22, 1965	army faction	successful
Dec. 17, 1967	army faction	successful

Date	Main Party	Outcome
July 12, 1969	army faction	failed
Oct. 21, 1969	army faction	failed
Dec. 10, 1969	army faction	successful
Feb. 28, 1972	army faction	failed
Oct. 26, 1972	army faction	successful
Jan. 21, 1975	army and political faction	failed
Jan. 16, 1977 *	[foreign-supported faction]	failed

Burundi

Oct. 19, 1965	army and political faction	failed
July 8, 1966	Prince plus army faction	successful
Nov. 28, 1966	Prime Minister plus army faction	successful
Nov. 1, 1976	army and tribal faction	successful

Central African Empire

| Jan. 1, 1966 | army faction | successful |
| April 12, 1969 | army faction | failed |

Chad

August 26, 1971	foreign-supported faction	failed
April 13, 1975	army faction	successful
March 31, 1977	army and tribal faction	failed

Comoros

August 3, 1975	army and political faction	successful
June 4, 1977	army and political faction	failed
May 13, 1978	foreign mercenaries	successful

Congo, People's Republic of

August 15, 1963	army and labour unions	successful
June 28-29, 1966	army and tribal faction	failed
August 3-31, 1968	army faction	successful
Sept. 4, 1968	army faction	successful
Nov. 8, 1969	army faction	failed
March 23, 1970	army faction	failed
Feb. 22, 1972	left-wing army faction	failed

* It is widely believed that this *coup* was simulated by President Mattneu Kerekou for internal political reasons.

Date	Main Party	Outcome
March 18, 1977	political faction	failed

Egypt

July 23, 1952	army faction	successful
Feb. 5, 1966	left-wing political faction	failed
Sept. 24, 1966	political faction	failed
August 27, 1967	army and political faction	failed
June 1, 1975	political faction	failed

Equatorial Guinea

March 21, 1969	army and political faction	failed

Ethiopia

Dec. 13-17, 1960	army faction	failed
Sept. 12, 1974	elements from three services	successful
Nov. 22-24, 1974	faction in ruling Military Council	successful
Feb. 3, 1977	faction in ruling Military Council	failed

Gabon

Feb. 17-18, 1964 *	army faction	failed

Ghana

Feb. 24, 1966	army faction	successful
April 17, 1967	army faction	failed
Jan. 13, 1972	army faction	successful
Jan. 15, 1972	army faction	failed

Guinea

Nov. 22, 1970	foreign-supported faction	failed
May 13, 1976	army and political faction	failed

Lesotho

Jan. 30, 1970	political faction	successful

Liberia

Feb. 5, 1963	political faction	failed

* The government of Leon Mba was briefly overthrown by a military coup, but was reinstated the next day when French troops intervened under the terms of a 1961 defense agreement [with France].

Date	Main Party	Outcome

Libya

Sept. 1, 1969	elements from three services	successful
Dec. 10, 1969	foreign-supported faction	failed
August 14, 1975	army faction	failed

Madagascar (Malagasy Republic)

April 1, 1971	left-wing army faction	failed
May 18, 1972	political faction	successful
Feb. 5-12, 1975	army faction	successful

Mali

Nov. 19, 1968	army faction	successful
April 7, 1971	army faction	failed

Mauritania

July 10, 1978	army faction	successful

Morocco

July 10, 1971	general's faction in army	failed
August 17, 1972	air force faction	failed

Mozambique

Dec. 17, 1975	army and police faction	failed

Niger

April 15, 1974	all forces	successful
August 2, 1975	army and political faction	failed
March 15, 1976	army and political faction	failed

Nigeria

Jan. 15, 1966	army faction	successful
July 29, 1966	northern army faction	successful
July 29, 1975	army faction	successful
Feb. 13, 1976	army faction	failed

Rwanda

July 5, 1973	army and police faction	successful

Seychelles

June 5, 1977	police and political faction	successful

Date	Main Party	Outcome
Sierra Leone		
March 23, 1967	army faction	successful
April 18, 1968	army faction	successful
Somalia		
Oct. 21, 1969	army and police faction	successful
April 21, 1970	army and political faction	failed
May 25, 1971	army and political faction	failed
April 9, 1978	army faction	failed
Sudan		
August 18, 1955	army and tribal faction	failed
Nov. 17, 1958	army faction	successful
Dec. 28, 1966	left-wing army faction	failed
May 25, 1969	left-wing army faction	successsful
July 19-22, 1971	left-wing army faction	failed
Sept. 5, 1975	army faction	failed
Feb. 2, 1977	air force faction	failed
Tanzania (Tanganyika and Zanzibar)		
Jan. 12, 1964 (Zanzibar)	political faction	successful
Jan. 20, 1964 (Tanganyika)	troop mutiny	failed
Togo		
Jan. 13, 1963	army and tribal faction	successful
Nov. 21-22, 1966	political faction	failed
Jan. 13, 1967	general's faction in army	successful
August 8, 1970	army and political faction	failed
Uganda		
Jan. 23, 1964	troop mutiny	failed
Jan. 25, 1971	army and police faction	successful
March 23, 1974	army faction	failed
Upper Volta		
Jan 3, 1966	army faction	successful

Date	Main Party	Outcome
Zaire		
Nov. 25, 1965	army faction	successful
May 30, 1966	political faction	failed
ASIA		
Afghanistan		
July 17, 1973	army and police	successful
Nov. 30, 1976	retired army officers	failed
April 27, 1978	army and air force	successful
Bangladesh		
August 15, 1975	army and political faction	successful
Nov. 7, 1975	army mutiny	failed
Oct. 2, 1977	army and air force faction	failed
Burma		
Sept. 26, 1958	army faction	successful
March 2, 1962	elements from three services	successful
July 24, 1974	left-wing political faction	failed
Cambodia (Dem. Kampuchea)		
March 18, 1970	elements from three services	successful
Indonesia		
Dec. 3, 1950	navy faction	failed
April 26, 1950	elements from two services	failed
Oct. 1, 1965	Communist Party	failed
Nov. 16, 1965	elements from three services	failed
Korea, Republic of		
Oct. 20, 1948	army faction	failed
May 16, 1961	elements from three services	successful
Laos		
August 9, 1960	neutralist army faction	successful
April 19, 1964	right-wing army faction	successful
Jan. 31, 1965	army and police faction	failed
Oct. 21, 1966	air force faction	failed
August 20, 1973	air force faction	failed

Date	Main Party	Outcome
Nepal		
Dec. 15, 1960	King plus army faction	successful
Pakistan		
Oct. 7-27, 1958	elements from three services	successful
July 5, 1977	elements from three services	successful
Sri Lanka		
Jan. 29, 1962	political faction	failed
Thailand		
Nov. 9, 1947	army faction	successful
June 29, 1951	navy faction	failed
Nov. 29, 1951	army faction	successful
Sept. 16, 1957	army faction	successful
Oct. 20, 1958	army faction	successful
Nov. 17, 1971	Prime Minister	successful
Feb. 24, 1976	army faction	failed
Oct. 20, 1976	elements from three services	successful
March 26, 1977	army and political faction	failed
Oct. 20, 1977	elements of three forces	successful
Vietnam		
Nov. 1-2, 1963	elements from three services	successful
Jan. 30, 1964	elements from three services	successful
Jan. 27, 1965	elements from three services	successful
Feb. 21, 1965	elements from three services	successful

LATIN AMERICA

Argentina		
Sept. 28, 1951	elements from three services	failed
June 16, 1955	navy faction	failed
Sept. 16, 1955	elements from three services	successful
Nov. 13, 1955	army faction	successful
June 13, 1960	army faction	failed
March 28, 1962	elements from three services	successful
August 8, 1962	troop mutiny	failed

Date	Main Party	Outcome
April 2, 1963	general's faction in army	failed
June 28, 1966	army and navy generals	successful
June 8, 1970	elements from three services	successful
March 23, 1971	elements from three services	successful
May 11, 1971	army and political faction	failed
Oct. 8, 1971	army faction	failed
March 1, 1974	police	failed
Dec. 18, 1975	right-wing air force faction	failed
March 24, 1976	elements from three services	successful

Bolivia

May 16, 1951	army and air force faction	successful
April 9, 1952	army and political faction	successful
Nov. 3, 1964	army and air force faction	successful
August 21, 1968	army faction	failed
Sept. 26, 1969	army and air force faction	successful
Oct. 6-7, 1970	army and air force faction	successful
Jan. 10, 1971	right-wing army faction	failed
Aug. 19-22, 1971	right-wing army faction	successful
May 17, 1972	left-wing political faction	failed
May 15, 1973	right-wing army faction	failed
June 5, 1974	army faction	failed
Dec. 9, 1977	army faction	failed
July 28, 1978	army and political faction	successful

Brazil

Oct. 29, 1945	elements from three services	successful
Nov. 11, 1955	army faction	successful
August 26, 1961	elements from three services	successful
April 1, 1964	elements from three services	successful

Chile

June 29, 1973	right-wing army and political faction	failed
Sept. 11, 1973	elements from three services	successful

Colombia

June, 13, 1953	elements from three services	successful

Date	Main Party	Outcome
May 10, 1957	elements from three services	successful
Cuba		
March 10, 1952	army faction	successful
Dominican Republic		
Jan. 13, 1962	army faction	failed
Sept. 25, 1963	army faction	successful
April 25, 1965	army and air force faction	successful
Nov. 26, 1965	right-wing army and political faction	failed
Ecuador		
March 14, 1947	elements from three forces	failed
August 23, 1947	elements from three services	successful
Sept. 1-3, 1947	elements from three services	successful
Nov. 7-9, 1961	elements from three services	successful
July 11, 1963	elements from three services	successful
March 29, 1966	political faction	successful
Feb. 15, 1972	elements from three services	successful
Sept. 1, 1975	military and political faction	failed
Jan. 11, 1976	elements from three services	successful
El Salvador		
Dec. 14, 1948	army faction	successful
Oct. 26, 1960	military and political faction	successful
Jan. 25, 1961	right-wing political	successful
March 25, 1972	army and political faction	failed
Guatemala		
July 9, 1949	army faction	failed
Jan. 20, 1955	political faction	failed
Oct. 25, 1957	elements from three services	successful
Nov. 13, 1960	left-wing army and political faction	failed
March 30, 1963	army faction	successful
Haiti		
Jan. 11, 1946	army faction	successful
May 10, 1950	army faction	successful

Date	Main Party	Outcome
August 5-7, 1963	armed political faction	failed

Honduras

Oct. 21, 1956	army and air force	successful
Oct. 3, 1963	army faction	successful
Dec. 3, 1972	army and air force faction	successful
April 22, 1975	army faction	successful
Oct. 21, 1977	right-wing political faction	failed

Nicaragua

May 26, 1947	army faction	successful
Jan. 22-23, 1967	right-wing army and political faction	failed

Panama

Nov. 20, 1949	police	successful
May 9, 1951	army and political faction	successful
Oct. 12, 1968	national guard	successful
Dec. 16, 1969	national guard faction	failed

Paraguay

March 7, 1947	army faction	failed
June 3, 1948	political party faction	successful
Dec. 30, 1948	political party faction	successful
Feb. 26, 1949	political party faction	successful
May 5, 1954	army faction	successful

Peru

Oct. 3, 1948	navy faction	failed
Oct. 27, 1948	right-wing army faction	successful
Feb. 16, 1956	right-wing army faction	failed
July 18, 1962	elements from three services	successful
March 3, 1963	elements from three services	successful
Oct. 3, 1968	elements from three services	successful
August 29, 1975	army faction	successful
July 9, 1976	right-wing army faction	failed

Trinidad-Tobago

April 21, 1970	army mutiny	failed

Venezuela

Nov. 23, 1948	army and political faction	successful

Date	Main Party	Outcome
Nov. 11, 1950	political faction	failed
Dec. 2, 1952	elements from three services	successful
June 24, 1960	foreign-supported faction	failed
May 4, 1962	right-wing navy faction	failed
June 3, 1962	left-wing navy faction	failed
Oct. 30, 1966	national guard faction	failed

MIDDLE EAST/SOUTHWEST ASIA

Cyprus

July 15, 1974	national guard	successful

Iraq

July 15, 1958	army faction	successful
March 8-9, 1959	left-wing army faction	failed
Feb. 8, 1963	army and air force faction	successful
Nov. 18, 1963	air force faction	successful
Sept. 17, 1965	army faction	failed
June 30, 1966	Nasserist army faction	failed
July 17, 1968	right-wing Baathist army faction	successful
Jan. 20, 1970	foreign-supported faction	failed
June 30, 1973	police and political faction	failed

Lebanon

Dec. 31, 1961	army and tribal faction	failed

Oman

July 23, 1970	Sultan's son plus palace guard	successful

Qatar

Feb. 22, 1972	royal faction	successful

Sharjah

Jan. 24, 1972	political faction	failed

Syria

March 30, 1949	army faction	successful
August 18, 1949	army faction	successful
Dec. 17, 1949	army faction	successful
Nov. 28, 1951	army faction	successful
Feb. 25, 1954	army faction	successful

Date	Main Party	Outcome
Sept. 28, 1961	army and political faction	successful
March 28, 1962	army faction	successful
April 1, 1962	Nasserist army faction	failed
March 8, 1963	left-wing army faction	successful
Feb. 23, 1966	left-wing Baathist army faction	successful
Sept. 8, 1966	army faction	failed
Feb. 28, 1969	army faction	successful
Nov. 13, 1970	right-wing Baathist army faction	successful

Turkey

May 21, 1960	elements from three services	successful
Feb. 27, 1962	army faction	failed
May 20, 1963	army and air force faction	failed
March 12, 1971*	general's faction in army	successful
March 2, 1975	army faction	failed

Yemen

Nov. 5, 1967	political faction	successful
March 2, 1968	left-wing political and tribal faction	failed
July 25, 1968	army faction	failed
Jan. 26, 1969	army faction	failed
June 13, 1974	army faction	successful
Oct. 11, 1977	army and political faction	failed

Yemen, Democratic

June 26, 1978	army faction	successful

EUROPE
Czechoslovakia

Feb. 21, 1948	Communist Party	successful

* Military leaders threatened to take over the government unless a strong coalition government was established to replace that of Prime Minister Suleyman Demirel. Prime Minister Nibat Erim established a new coalition government two weeks later.

Date	Main Party	Outcome
Greece		
April 21, 1967	right-wing army faction	successful
Dec. 13, 1967	King	failed
May 24, 1973	naval mutiny	failed
Nov. 25, 1973	army and naval faction	successful
Portugal		
Jan. 1, 1962	army mutiny	failed
April 25, 1974	army and political faction	successful
Sept. 24, 1974	army faction	failed
March 11, 1975	right-wing air force faction	failed
July 31, 1975	elements from three services	failed
Nov. 25, 1975	left-wing paratroopers	failed

TABLE III *The Efficiency of the* Coup d'État, *1945-64*

Outcome as a Function of Conflict Type

Type	Conflict Continuing	Inconclusive	Lost	Half and Half	Won	Don't Know
civil disorder	4	25	47	26	18	3
coup d'état	0	0	24	2	62	
military revolt	0	3	17	0	3	
military/insurrection	0	4	33	8	2	•
guerrilla war	5	2	6	4	8	1
civil war	1	2	4	4	6	
border conflict	8	14	3	3	0	
limited war	0	1	3	1	1	
covert invasion	2	5	1	1	1	
blockage, etc.	0	0	2	2	0	
threat	1	1	0	0	1	
	21	57	146	51	102	4

TABLE IV. *The Frequency of the* Coup d'État
Time Distribution of Type of Conflict 1945–64 (based on starting date of conflict)
Time Periods: A 1 January 1946–30 April 1952
                B 1 May 1952–31 August 1958
                C 1 September 1958–31 December 1964

Type of Conflict	A	B	C
Internal:			
civil disorder	35	32	56
localized internal:			
coup d'état	25	18	44
military revolt/mutiny	8	6	17
insurrection	15	12	12
widespread internal:			
guerrilla war	11	10	5
civil war	4	7	6
International:			
conventional:			
border conflict	7	12	9
limited war	3	2	1
other:			
covert invasion	6	3	7
blockade, etc.	2	1	1
threat	0	2	1
TOTAL:	116	105	159

Index